Spirit of Sail

CLIPPERS, WINDJAMMERS AND TALL SHIPS.

TEXT BY JOHN DYSON
PHOTOGRAPHS BY PETER CHRISTOPHER

The Kingswood Press
an imprint of William Heinemann Ltd.
10 Upper Grosvenor Street, London W1X 9PA

LONDON   MELBOURNE
JOHANNESBURG   AUCKLAND

Copyright text © 1987 by John Dyson

*Copyright photographs © 1987 by Peter
Christopher*

First published 1987

*Originally published in Canada by
Key Porter Books Limited, Toronto*

ISBN 0 434 98119 2

*Design: Brant Cowie/Artplus Ltd.
Typesetting: Imprint Typesetting
Printing and Binding: Scanner Art Services Ltd.
Printed and bound in Hong Kong
87 88 89 90 6 5 4 3 2 1*

PHOTO CREDITS
*All photographs in this book are by Peter
Christopher with the following exceptions:*

   *David MacGregor Collection: pages 24,
     27, 66, 71, 79, 115 (top), 128*
   *National Maritime Museum Greenwich:
     endpapers and pages 20, 23, 29, 32, 76,
     115 (bottom), 117, 125*
   Nautical Photo Agency: page 28
   New-York Historical Society: page 19
   Popperfoto: pages 67, 69, 75, 123

For our children

PAGE 1: *The sailing ship in her natural element, where the chart shows nothing but hundreds of miles of open ocean: the Polish three-master* Dar Mlodziezy *surges through heavy seas in the north-west Atlantic.*

PAGE 2: *There's nothing like the sight of a line of Tall Ships to take the heart back a few decades. Berthed in the St. Lawrence River at Quebec City, these ships have gathered to celebrate the 450th anniversary of the arrival of the first Europeans in what is now Canada.*

THIS PAGE: *Cadets dress their ships in flags prior to a festival of youth and sail in Amsterdam.*

PAGES 6 AND 7: : *In heavy fog off New England, the crew of* Dar Mlodziezy *lays aloft to stow sail; the ship's 248-foot masts are the tallest of any ship afloat.*

PAGES 8 AND 9: *The complex web of mast, spar, sail, and rigging is the sailor's domain and every bit is independently adjustable. Working smartly in unison as* Dar Mlodziezy *takes part in a sail-past at Sydney, Nova Scotia, cadets lay out on the yards and stand by for the order to furl sail.*

PAGES 10 AND 11: *Setting an upper topgallant in the U.S. Coast Guard barque* Eagle, *a girl cadet first scrambles up the rigging to release the gaskets tying the sail to the spar. Next, crew members on deck, hauling on long ropes, will hoist the spar aloft, stretching the sail to the wind.*

Contents

Introduction

"Would'st thou,"—so the helmsman answered,
"Learn the secret of the sea?
Only those who brave its dangers
Comprehend its mystery!"
HENRY WADSWORTH LONGFELLOW

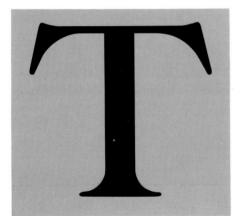HE NORWEGIAN square-rigged sailing ship *Christian Radich* dead-pegged into a North Sea gale. With only jibs and stay-sails hoisted, we drove relentlessly into steep, close waves. The rigging shivered from the pounding. The bows tossed solid water up to the gray sky and the wind blasted it like grapeshot along the deck. But for every hard-won mile the windage of three masts and masses of cordage caused a mile to be lost. In four miserable days we made little ground.

Crack! The flying jib split in half. The first mate, a wide-shouldered Viking, shouted for help. Though wan with exhaustion and seasickness two young crewmen followed him out along the wildly plunging bowsprit. Sitting astride the spar that jutted ahead of the ship like a spear, the three fought to save the torn and rattling sail before it was whipped to tatters by the gale.

Suddenly the 241-foot ship seemed to hang in space as an immense trough yawned beneath her bow. Then she dropped. The bowsprit speared into a green wall. In the instant before I was myself engulfed in sheets of spray, I glimpsed three pairs of seaboots jutting out of the smother, their soles pointed to the sky. Then the bowsprit burst clear of the water and soared upward, the sailors hugging it for their lives.

With fingers, knees, teeth, and guts, those men fisted the sail into submission then lashed it down. When they wriggled aft and regained the safety of the foredeck, I saw grins charting great-circle routes around their chapped, dripping, triumphant faces. They were wet to the skin, miserably cold, and had been hugely scared. Yet they were jubilant.

We may romance all we want about "the wheel's kick and the wind's song," as John Masefield put it, but these young sailors had tasted the reality of seafaring. The sea had tested their mettle. It had racked every sinew and rattled them to their nerve-ends, but they had survived. Moreover, they had got the job done and were laughing about it. This was the spirit of sail.

Spirit of sail is what drove the wonderful racing clipper ships across the oceans more than a century ago. Spirit of sail inspired young adventurers to sweat brutish, rust-streaked windjammers around Cape Horn in days when there were plenty of easier berths available at sea but none more exciting. What the world lost with the end of commercial sailing ships is more than the dramatic spectacle of white canvas flowering from every spar of a tall ship. More, too, than the nautical craftsmanship that went into every knot and splice of her. When steamers and motor ships came close to wiping the sailing ship from the face of the ocean, the world lost what men did in them. We lost the challenges and joys of working high canvas — the spirit of sail.

Though not quite lost. Today, the spirit of sail is that self-assured, capable look you can't help noticing in the tanned faces of all the young crews ranged on the decks of the fleet of Tall Ships when they congregate in ports of the world for festivals of sail.

The millions of spectators who throng these events wonder at the fascinating webs of masts, spars, and rigging. For the moment the ship is in repose, a bird with her head under her folded wing. The beautiful vessel has something about her: a promise of new beginnings, an air of bright and high-handed adventure. Perhaps visitors catch an echo of "the grand oratorio of rope and wire singing, booming, humming, and whining" in the winds. But few of those who cram the shoreline to admire the beauty of Tall Ships under sail are lucky enough to see and *know* a sailing ship in her natural element, where the chart shows hundreds of miles of nothing but open ocean.

In *Spirit of Sail* we have attempted to make good this lack, showing what happens when the Tall Ships stretch their wings to the wind and flee to the environment they know best.

Peter Christopher
John Dyson
1987

FOLLOWING PAGES: A pearly dawn in St. Malo, France, heralds quiet weather for the start of the Tall Ships Race across the Atlantic to Bermuda.

1 *Spirit of the Clippers*

A sailing ship voyage is a kind of fight.
ALAN VILLIERS

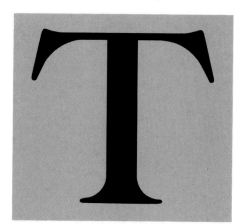

HE CLIPPER, as old sailors would say, was a ship to grapple with every element but fire. She sailed like the wind, heaved-to like a duck, and ran till all was blue. In the whole history of navigation nothing excelled her dash and good looks — the slender hull, springy as a sea hollow; the three tall masts slightly raked to give her a youthful look, hungry for action; the great blade of her bow, curved and sharp, scattering flying fish as it scythed blue water.

While other vessels hugged the shore and plunged awkwardly on their anchors awaiting favorable winds, the clipper might be glimpsed making sail and thrashing eagerly away into the squalls, outward bound. The harder it blew the harder she cracked on, a tremble in every knot, stitch, and splice of her. Through trade-wind latitudes she cut a scintillating furrow, sails piled up like a thundercloud, every stitch-hole an elongated slot through which splinters of sunshine glanced. Then she lifted to the long greasy rollers of the southern ocean and drove down the roaring forties with albatrosses soaring stiff-winged in her wake. When the headlands of tropical islands stretched out, black in the moonlight, the clipper ghosted close along the shore to catch the night breezes, the watch listening to the jabber of jungle monkeys.

The clipper ship's trade was distance. She was not capacious so all her profit lay in speed. She made her name on grand globe-girdling passages,

One of the few training ships that does not head for warmer climes in winter, Gorch Fock II *remains in the North Sea where cadets need all their stamina and courage when working aloft.*

sailing nearly twice as fast as anything else afloat, even steamers. To the far coast of a continent she freighted provisions and hardware for the thousands of hopefuls flocking to the goldfields, sailing from New York to California by way of Cape Horn in a hundred days or less. To goldfields on the far side of the world she carried diggers and bullwhackers, Australia bound. In a "celestial kingdom" on the far side of civilization, the clipper loaded fragrant cargoes of pekoe and bohea teas, then raced them to London. Plunging through seas infested with pirates and uncharted reefs, then charging across two oceans by way of the Cape of Good Hope, the clippers tore more than halfway around the globe only to reach the English Channel within sight of each other.

In those days when locomotives were a novelty, roads were as rough as the sea, and all the world's trade traveled on the wind's back, the breathtaking nerve and splendor of clipper ships caught the popular imagination as space flights do in modern times. When clippers were sighted racing wing to wing up to London, more bets were said to ride on the outcome than on the Derby. Images of these most glorious and romantic days of racing sail persist in the poems and prose of John Masefield and Joseph Conrad and in the paintings of the famous tea clippers adorning everything from jigsaw puzzles to tea caddies. The brief but glorious days of the racing clipper are perceived as the most romantic era of passage-making, the very essence of the spirit of sail. And it is this spirit that endures when today's fleets of Tall Ships congregate for celebrations of youth and sail.

Fabricated in timber, iron, canvas, and hemp, the beauty of the clipper ship bears comparison with that of the finest cathedrals. A clipper was certainly a ship worth looking at, but she was designed no more for the sake of art than for the glory of God.

The elegance of the clipper ship had but one function: expedience. In the middle of the nineteenth century, ships no longer had to carry guns, except against pirates, because the major nations were at peace. An industrial age had dawned. New territories were being claimed and pioneered. There was a drive to conquer distance, and this required speed. Fast passages commanded high freights, because speed was a commodity shippers would pay for.

For nearly two centuries, up to 1849, navigation laws had required British cargoes to be carried on British keels. None sailed faster than a majestic plod, and sail was reduced at sundown for comfort, though it mattered little because cargo was in no hurry and passengers were concerned only with traveling in style and safety. It was nothing to spend a hundred and fifty days on a passage from China, a time crack clippers soon cut by a third.

The fast vessels of the day were sloops, cutters, and schooners hardly larger than modern yachts. One of the speediest was the Baltimore "clipper," originally developed from French schooners and refined, first for privateering during the War of 1812 then to trade slaves. When the smoke cleared after the Battle of Waterloo in 1815, ending the prolonged wars between Great Britain and France, swift and graceful little craft were developed for a variety of purposes, such as eluding pirate galleys to smuggle opium into China, but they were small. Even the racy Yankee

Fine lines and a sharp bow that sliced through the water were characteristic of the clipper ship: Rainbow, *built in New York was an early example.*

packets driven hard across the Atlantic with passengers and mail to make twenty-three days from New York to Liverpool, forty days on the return, were less than a hundred feet long.

The clipper ship would be a happy combination of the twin virtues of British capaciousness and American speed, and it came about thanks to gold and tea.

One of the first true clipper ships was the *Rainbow*, built in New York in 1845. In place of the traditional round, "apple-cheek" bows that pushed water ahead, a knifelike stem cut through the waves and the concave lines of the forward part of the vessel pushed the water aside. The stern was given an elegant taper, like a champagne glass. The hull, slender rather than squat, gained in length what it lacked in breadth. It cut more cleanly through the water so cargo was delivered faster and with less labor and strain. The clipper was a ship capable of seeking out favorable winds, while the old full-bodied vessels had to wait for them.

Hardly had the new concept been tested, its weak points rectified by trial and error, than gold was found lying in the dust near a distant bay in what was then Mexico. In 1848, four vessels arrived in San Francisco; next year no fewer than 775 ships landed passengers. With thousands of gold diggers braving thirst, cold, and Indian attack as they streamed across the continent, the need for provisions and equipment in California was desperate. A single barrel of flour could fetch forty-four dollars. For freight, the sea route via Cape Horn was the only way to go. Large, fast vessels were required to carry it. And the ship for the job had just been perfected.

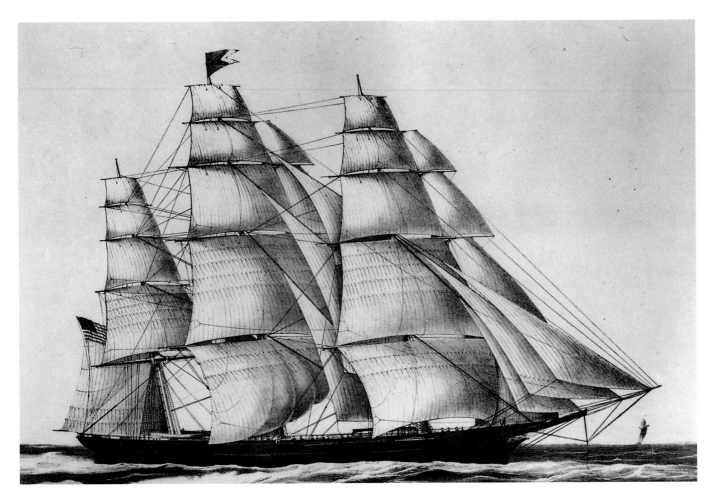

Between 1850 and 1854, New York and Boston constructed no fewer than one hundred and sixty Yankee clippers for the California run. The zenith came in 1853 when forty-eight were launched. The profits of a quick passage to California were so substantial that many ships paid all the costs of their construction on their maiden voyage. But when the wild rush to the goldfields began to subside, many went on across the Pacific to load China tea, first for New York then for London.

With the Opium War of 1842, Great Britain had forced China to open five new ports to foreign trade. Suddenly a great deal of tea was available, all levels of Britain's industrialized society were able to afford it, and demand outstripped the ability of Britain's own lumbering "tea wagons" to deliver. In drawing rooms and front parlors it became fashionable to drink the freshest tea from the first vessel of the season to arrive, and high premiums were paid to that ship. When Britain's protectionist navigation laws were repealed in 1849, opening her trade to ships of any flag, the Yankee clippers got their chance. The *Oriental* sailed into the Thames in December 1850, the Stars and Stripes whipping in the breeze and cocking a snook at the entire British mercantile empire. Despite the head winds of the monsoon, she had run from China in ninety-seven days.

At the same time, American steamers were setting the pace on the Atlantic run. A Yankee schooner called *America* had whopped British yachtsmen in their very stronghold, sailing off with a cup that would become the most famous and bitterly contested trophy in history. The British quickly set about catching up.

The Flying Cloud, *built in New York in 1851, twice sailed by way of Cape Horn to California in 89 days, a record that has never been beaten under sail.*

In New York alone, ten thousand shipwrights and riggers were turning out new clippers on the banks of the East River; the same number were at work in Boston. Soon the two ports were each launching up to forty new clippers a year. Such was public interest in them that *Staghound*, built in sixty days, was cheered by no fewer than fifteen thousand people as she slid down the ways into the water. News of the crack Yankee clippers was on everybody's lips on both sides of the Atlantic. In 1851, *Typhoon*, the largest merchant ship ever seen in Liverpool, set a new transatlantic record of thirteen days, ten hours. The magnificent *Flying Cloud* covered 374 nautical miles in a single day, forty-two miles better than the fastest steamer on the Atlantic run. When most ships were taking two hundred days to reach California, and the record was one hundred and twenty days, *Flying Cloud* sailed through the Golden Gate just eighty-nine days out, making the first transcontinental link in less than three months. Though equalled twice, once by the same ship, this record was never beaten under sail.

The flying clippers carried comparatively large crews because manpower was inexpensive. A shipmaster could afford to hang on to his sail until his masts and spars were bending under the strain because he knew he had muscle and hands enough to handle it.

With strong men in command, all with names to make and records to break, it is hardly surprising that rivalry was intense. When a far-off dazzling speck grew into a cloud of canvas — a rival clipper on a parallel track — no effort was spared to crack on sail. No harbor yacht race was contested with hotter blood than the California clipper races round Cape Horn.

In 1852 *Stornoway* and *Chrysolite*, the first two real British clippers, sailed together from the Chinese port of Whampoa, near Canton, and raced in company for days, the latter's captain remaining on deck day and night in a deck chair lashed to the skylight. He reached Liverpool in one hundred and five days, three days before his rival docked in London, and landed the first of the season's teas ahead of the Americans.

With abundant supplies of inexpensive softwood, the United States soon had a great number of very large clippers, while Britain had relatively few. But hard driving under a mass of sail imposed stresses and strains that timber could not withstand. Also, Yankee ships quickly became sluggish because the soft timbers absorbed water.

In Britain, tools, canvas, and copper sheathing were less expensive and cordage was superior. But softwood hardly existed, while hardwood was scarce and costly. Shipbuilders therefore committed themselves to mastery of iron. It was years before they perfected riveting, the bending of iron frames, and the rolling of iron plates in long lengths. There were also practical problems with iron-built ships, such as ventilation and the vast amounts of weed that grew on the hull in tropical waters.

The builders persisted, however, especially with large vessels and those driven by steam, and through their technical accomplishment Great Britain regained her mastery of world sea trade. One of the first successful iron clippers was *Lord of the Isles*, launched in Greenock, Scotland, in 1852, and so fine-lined, causing her to drive through waves rather than over them, that her crew christened her the "diving bell." In 1856 she departed from Foochow, in China, one day after the American barque *Maury*. Both arrived off the Thames on the same morning and the Yankee was ten minutes in front at Gravesend. But the British ship had the smarter tug and was first into the dock.

Meanwhile, another gold strike was helping to make the middle years of the nineteenth century the most exciting and prosperous that sailing ships would ever know. Gold in lumps was being dug out of the raw earth in the hills behind Port Phillip Bay, near what is now the city of Melbourne, Australia. There was no question of traveling overland or by steamer. All passengers, supplies, and mails were transported to the diggings under sail, and it was sail that brought the gold home to Great Britain, along with ever-increasing cargoes of baled wool.

Both to and from Australia, the traditional route for sailing ships was by way of the Cape of Good Hope. Duration of passage was typically one hundred and twenty days. But clipper ships cut that time nearly in half. Outward bound to Australia, they turned well south of the Cape and headed across the bottom of the world to "run their easting" in the powerful winds and wild seas of the south latitudes known as "the roaring forties." Running homeward, they continued around the globe in the same direction, again looking for strong stern winds in the world's loneliest ocean, then turned Cape Horn and headed up the Atlantic.

The stronger and more reliable winds of high latitudes in the southern ocean were a better test of speed than the fickle doldrum breezes and contrary monsoons in the China trade. Racing home, the wool clipper, a stronger, heavier type of ship developed for the Australia trade, made some astonishing passages. Under the hard-driving Captain "Bully" Forbes, the Boston-built *Lightning* logged 436 miles during twenty-four hours of a southerly gale. No steamer would come within a hundred miles of this performance for the next quarter century. It is probably still the fastest day's run ever made under sail.

The U.S. softwood clippers were too big to excel in this trade. There was not enough wool and tallow to fill them, and they took such a hammering from the weather that repair bills were prohibitive. Yankee ships were hit hard by the shipping glut that followed the end of the Crimean War in 1857, and were hit again by financial depression at home; then the American Civil War finished them off. In Britain, iron construction made great strides, free trade was generating a new spirit of endeavor, and new tonnage laws encouraged a more scientific approach to design. Many were the varieties of the fast and beautiful birds of passage whose voyages followed those of the Yankee clippers into the record books. In 1863, from a yard at Greenock, on the River Clyde, in Scotland, emerged the pattern of ship that was to become almost legendary as the perfect combination of cargo capacity, sea-kindliness, speed, and beauty.

First of the breed was *Taeping*, a "composite" vessel built with an iron frame and a timber planking. Though not new, this type of construction, had never been used to such pleasing effect. The iron frame prevented the hull from twisting, and it removed the need for massive close-spaced timbers. The design was tighter and less expensive, and permitted a longer ship for the weight. The planking of greenheart and teak was

The great tea race of 1866: Taeping (left) *and* Ariel, *having left the China coast astern at almost the same moment three months before, surge bow-to-bow up the English Channel at 14 knots with every sail set. Lithograph by T.G. Dutton.*

sheathed in copper to prevent the bottom from growing weed. The timbered hull stowed a larger cargo, did not "sweat" with sudden temperature changes as iron did, and was greatly preferred for a tea cargo, whose value depended on its taste and fragrance. Iron masts and lower spars with wire rigging saved weight aloft yet provided sufficient strength for nearly thirty thousand square feet of sail.

Immediately fashionable, the "Greenock model" was copied by other yards on the Clyde. All were remarkably similar in appearance, though there were numerous variations in detail and in the form of the underwater hull. In all, scarcely thirty were built, yet they brought the commercial sailing ship to its highest pitch of performance and loveliness and plied a trade that was in the forefront of the public imagination. Clippers of many kinds had carried tea from China, but these were *the* China tea clippers.

Slim and graceful, a yachtlike vessel of neat appearance, the China tea clipper was of medium size, typically around 190 feet, with bowsprit and jibboom jutting some seventy feet ahead of the stem. The sail plan went for spread rather than hoist: masts were not enormously high but carried very wide yards. She was low in the water, her bulwarks rather low for elegance though this greatly increased the danger from seas breaking inboard. Decks were clear for working the ship. When *Ariel* ran her easting down, the crew built a temporary breakwater amidships to protect wheel, binnacles, and skylight from the water scooped up by the bows and sent surging aft along the deck.

For a brief, glorious period, through the 1860s and a few years beyond, the races between these perfect little ships heading home from China with the new season's tea — leaving Foochow at the end of May and docking some ninety-five days and sixteen thousand sea miles later — were a public spectacle. How exciting it must have been to encounter one of these white-winged beauties at full charge.

The most famous of the tea races was *Ariel*'s battle against *Taeping* in 1866. It was quite usual for rival tea clippers to leave different ports in

China several days apart and, approaching the English coast three months later, to see each other's topsails catching the sunlight in the distance.

In 1869, when three clippers arrived on the same day, *Leander* paced a Liverpool cargo steamer across the Indian Ocean and beat her to Mauritius. But the encounter was a sinister omen. For just at that time, the Suez Canal was being opened.

Steamers had been voyaging home from China via the Cape in eighty days but needed to carry so much coal for their boilers that little room was left for any cargo except passengers and gold. When the canal opened, they had a direct route to the East, and with new compound engines soon cut the trip to thirty-two days.

The "dirty ditch" dealt a knockout blow to the China clippers. Their wings clipped so they could be run by smaller crews, the loveliest of all sailing ships dispersed into other trades, then vanished. Many of them met ignoble ends. *Chrysolite* was wrecked in Madagascar with a cargo of bullocks; *Stornoway* foundered in the North Sea; *Staghound* burned to the waterline; *Surprise* was sunk by a drunken Japanese pilot; *Fiery Cross*, *Taeping*, and *Serica* were wrecked in the China Sea; *Ariel* was pooped and lost in the southern ocean. Others were cut down by steamers, converted into coal hulks, or simply disappeared with all hands. A dry-docked museum piece in London, England, today only *Cutty Sark* survives.

Clipper ships were dead, but the spirit of sail still flourished. A new age of sail was dawning.

Timber meets iron on the high seas: Robinson Crusoe *(left) was a typical wooden ship built in 1862 while* Roodee *was built of iron the following year for the same owner. Painting by Samuel H. Wilson.*

2 The Blue-Water Life

The sailor is frankness, the landsman is finesse.
HERMAN MELVILLE

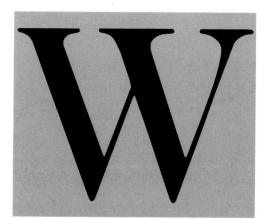

WATER HISSES in misty veils from the hurtling blade of the ship's bow. Flying fish whirring on silver wings dart away over waves of lovely indigo. Foam swirls along the shining black planks, converging beneath the tuck in a wake that points a crooked, scintillating finger at the sunrise. Filling an azure sky dappled with puffy clouds, tier after tilting tier of stiffly trembling sail gleams in translucent curves. The breeze is just strong enough to raise white horses and stream your hair, its melody not so much consciously heard as felt in the bones. The odd burst of spray dries the instant it strikes the hot deck, and leaves a salty crust. As the sun climbs higher, bubbling the pitch in the deck seams, barefooted sailors hop between stepping stones of shade.

The forceful, reliable trade winds fanning across the empty expanses of great oceans were God's gift to the perfection of sail. The sails hardly needed to be touched, except to harden in the ropes at dawn. Logging mile after easy mile with nothing around but air and sea, working in the centuries-old routine of "watch and watch" as soft tropical nights followed brilliant days, it seemed the ship would sail on for ever. This was the life for which sailors returned again and again to the sea. There was no peace in the world, they said, except in a sailing ship.

Through the middle decades of the nineteenth century, when the Yankee clippers, and then the China tea clippers of Great Britain, were the epitome of speed and grace under sail and steamships were yet to make an industrial treadmill of ocean voyaging, there was no shortage of inexpensive manpower. A crack ship never lacked a good crew.

A well-manned ship was a captain's special pride. He might be stuck with the shape of the hull and could adjust its trim only by shifting cargo. But the complex web of mast, spar, sail, and rigging was his domain. Every bit was independently adjustable. Profound technical skill and experience were required to knit those miles of cordage and acres of canvas into a single interacting and powerful driving engine. At the same time, the wind was constantly shifting direction and varying in strength. Sailcloth stretched, ropes shrank with wetness or fell slack in the sun. Keeping this engine tuned to its finest pitch, the whole rig driving with maximum power, was the shipmaster's obsession and he had only the brawn and skill of his crew with which to do it.

A clipper ship's crew, comprising about forty seamen and boys as well as "idlers," such as the carpenter ("Chips"), sailmaker ("Sails"), and cook ("Doctor"), who worked daylight hours and served no night watches, was accommodated in the forward part of the ship. The men were said to be sailing "before the mast." The captain and his two or three mates lived aft in relatively comfortable cabins grouped around a central saloon, generally with a large table and upholstered benches placed beneath an overhead skylight.

The fo'c'sle was a triangular compartment, usually unheated and unventilated, with bare wooden shelves on which the sailor spread his straw mattress and ringbolts in the floor to which he lashed the sea chest that contained his few possessions and gave him a chair to sit on. It was the liveliest and wettest part of the ship. In bad weather a foot or more of water surged from one side to the other as the ship rolled. To save cargo space below, crews of clippers often lived in a deckhouse forward, also called the fo'c'sle. Only in the last days of sail was a ship built with a crew's bathroom. You washed in a bucket of salt water or in a doldrums rainsquall. Sailors provided their own little comforts such as soap, fork, blanket, and oilskins. Basic clothing was sold at exorbitant prices from the captain's "slop chest."

Work in a sailing ship was never done, yet it had a pleasing simplicity and rhythm. The crew had two functions. One was to work the ship and make her go. The other was to work in the ship at the many skilled tasks that kept her taut and seaworthy.

As the ship made her departure, her men were divided into two teams, called watches, named for the two sides of the ship. By custom, the port watch was led by the mate and looked after the forward end of the ship and the foremast while the starboard watch, under the second mate, worked the main and mizzen masts. All hands were called on deck to set sails and cope with emergency situations. At other times the ship went into "watch and watch" routine: one watch carried out duties on deck such as steering, lookout, and handling the sails while the other slept, ate, or did ship's work.

Riggers' work aloft was the task in which seamen took the greatest pleasure and pride. A good sailor knew every knot, bend, and splice and could select the right one for the job as instinctively as he blinked in the

The "idlers" had special jobs. They did not stand watches but worked all day and stayed in their bunks at night unless all hands were called. They are the bosun (left) with his marline spike, "Chips" the carpenter (standing), "Sails" the sailmaker (right), and "Engines" (foreground) who looked after the small steam engine used to drive a winch on deck for handling cargo.

rain. In his big callused fingers the stiff manila hemp became as malleable as silk; splices and servings were crafted as artistically as any embroidery. A man who called himself "able seaman" could reeve a tackle of any given power, turn up a shroud, turn in a deadeye and join the two ends of a rough old hawser with a splice so smooth it was hardly visible. He could side-seam, repair, or cut sails for the sailmaker, put a clew in a square sail, or work a cringle into a leech-rope. As efficiently as any ship's carpenter, he could fish a broken spar, or rough out a new one.

In wooden ships rigged with ropes of natural fibers, maintenance was endless and demanded a high level of technical craftsmanship. The constant enemy was chafe. Any two ropes that crossed soon sawed each other through. Lines rubbing on canvas frayed it to pieces. In iron-hulled ships with wire rigging, however, maintenance was largely a painting job and sailors grew to loathe the chipping hammer with which they beat at bubbles of rust. Tedious days were spent rubbing deck planks and woodwork with sand and canvas to make it smooth, disagreeable work in cold weather. Tarring down was the dirtiest job. Sitting in a loop of rope, you lowered yourself down the full height of a stay and smeared it with a sticky coat of black lead and tallow.

Standing a "trick" at the wheel on a starry night, the ship snoring along in a warm wind, was a delight. The compass was bathed in a dim glow but you glanced at it only occasionally, to check the bearings of the star you chose to steer by. But in heavy weather, steering could be a nightmare. Forget John Masefield's notions of "the wheel's kick and the

ABOVE: Windjammer Garthsnaid, *built 1892, running in heavy weather, a hand to the lee wheel and a big sea piling up astern.*

RIGHT: Heaving the log in Garthsnaid: *while a sand-glass measures 28 seconds precisely, a line with knots tied at measured intervals is allowed to reel out astern. The number of knots passing through the mate's hand indicates the vessel's speed, each knot representing one nautical mile per hour.*

wind's song." The wheel's kick was a killer. It could throw a man clean over the spokes, landing him in the scuppers with broken bones or killing him, while the ship took charge of herself and went into a wild broach until she lay across the waves, seas smashing over her, men washed overboard, in deadly peril of losing her masts.

The captain of a sailing ship was absolute master of everything that fell under his eye, except the weather. In law and in fact he was second in command only to God. He was a man to take a three-day turn of driving his ship through a spell of ugly weather without turning a hair. His professional reputation as a fast passage-maker depended on his carrying every scrap of muslin his masts could hold. He would crack on until masts bent like fishing rods, but a good master seldom lost a spar. He was expected to be bold but never reckless. To undersail his ship lost time, to oversail her cost damage. He was expected to seek out the best winds without the aid of weather forecasts, and good masters knew where to look for them.

The road to promotion began when the brow-beaten ship's boy was made "ordinary" then "able" seaman. To become second mate, the first foothold on the ladder to command, you would have to be the kind of man always first to take hold when there was a job to be done; a sailing ship was no place for poop ornaments.

In day-work, the second mate instructed and supervised seamen. He took charge of the ship during his watch but the mate took over when all

The officers of the Brilliant, *a four-masted barque, photographed soon after the turn of the century. Captain T.C. Carlton (with white beard) is flanked by his mates with the apprentices in front.*

hands were called. The mate's job was to keep the ship functioning in every respect. While the captain was concerned with the ship's place in the world, his brain focused outboard, the second in command looked inboard and directed the world within the ship's bulwarks. When the captain decided on more sail, or less, it was the mate who saw the command properly executed. He was a vigilant and active character, a good judge of sail-trim and rigging, and capable of handling men.

The shipmaster was perhaps the most solitary of professional men. He was cut off from ordinary life by the sea and isolated from his shipmates by his rank and responsibilities. Yet a large measure of the spirit of the ship depended on him. Success required a special character of man.

Compared with the narrow toilsome lives of those ashore, sailoring always seemed romantic. There were hard times in all walks of life but the young sailor at least was spared the grimness of mill work or the penny-pinched livelihood of a farmhand. He sewed his tobacco pouch from the webbed foot of an albatross caught south of the Cape. In doldrum calms he joined in the sport of hauling a great shark out of the depths, nailing its tail to the jibboom to bring wind. His mother and sweetheart were kept supplied with a succession of gifts from exotic ports of call: embroidered silk and carved ivories from China, grebe muffs from Archangel, guava jelly from the Caribbean, a lump of coral from a Pacific reef for a doorstop, a chattering parrot bargained from a bumboat as his ship glided through the Sunda Strait on the breaths of a tropical night.

At sea there was always a better chance than elsewhere of improving his lot. With nothing to his name but strong arms and a robust constitution, a young man could work his way up in a few short years from cabin boy to shipmaster, to shipowner, as many then did.

Released from the cough syrups and mufflers of his mother's care, a lad would find himself washing (if he bothered) in a pail of rainwater while hailstones lashed the nape of his neck. The way ahead would seem miserably darkened by seasickness, discipline, and discomfort.

After a while, though, he would come to terms with the dank fo'c'sle where he lived, which had a smell he could almost lean on. He would adjust to the ship's lively motion over the sea and the hard routine of watch and watch: hardly four hours of sleep a night, and that often in wet clothes in a wet bunk. And in time, perched astride a yardarm swinging giddily through the sky, he would become aware (perhaps without voicing it in his thoughts) that only one thing had any importance under the sun and that was his ship and shipmates.

The spirit that existed between shipmates was the true romance of the sea, and remains so among the crews of young people sailing Tall Ships today. It is more than the close-knit family feeling of a congenial and high-spirited bunch of people in a happy ship: its essence is the comradeship founded on the trust that exists between seamen. A sailor stepped out on a footrope in the certain knowledge that the shipmates who fitted it had done the job properly. As he pinned his faith — his very life — on others, so they put their trust in him.

At sea, social background, upbringing, book learning, and even nationality and language had no relevance. Any window dressing or dry rot in a person's character was quickly exposed. You did your job, you put

some polish on it, and by this alone you were judged and trusted. The experience of shared dangers and discomforts forged a unique bond.

But the sea itself was always a grimly unromantic environment. The new hand would come to love ships (everything over which you sweat blood looks beautiful) but, like all his shipmates, he would soon fear and loathe the sea. They called it "the gray widow-maker."

Every voyage in a sailing ship was a kind of fight, men against the sea. The fight was unequal, for human nature was seldom prepared for the sea's unmitigated treachery: the squall that beat hissing and roaring out of the night, the uncharted reef avoided only because a bleary lookout happened to sight a spurt of spume tossed into the wind, the harrowing landfall made in a gale when a ship narrowly escaped being cast up on the shores of home.

Hardships were confined to certain latitudes where wind and weather probed for a man's weaknesses, but his victory over them was a kind of triumph. Storms, waves, and other perils of the mariner seemed terrible only to those on shore, who never saw them. The sailor took in his stride the risk of falling out of the rigging or being washed overboard. No pity for the man whose life was miraculously saved by the belly of a sail as he plunged off the yard: just a laugh and he got back on the job.

The real hardships of the sailor's calling were the long periods of isolation termed by Joseph Conrad "the hours spent between." Removal from ordinary life crippled the sailor's ability to cope with it. On land he appeared uncouth and inept, and his work skills had no value. No choice for him but to return to the life he knew. Dr. Samuel Johnson knew little about ships, as his famous dictionary reveals, but he was right about sailors: "Men go to sea before they know the unhappiness of that way of life," he wrote, "and when they have come to know it, they cannot escape from it."

On land, sailors were reckless with money: they survived the sea only to drown in port. But after months of isolation the trusting sailor would quickly fall victim to the sharks on land. Ironically, in many ports of the world the whole system of manning ships depended on it. When a ship made port after a long voyage the runners from different boarding houses swarmed aboard and tempted the crew ashore with offers of booze, women, and good times. Shipmasters were powerless against it.

Later, reduced to insensibility by liquor, the hapless sailor would be heaved unconscious aboard an outward-bounder, sold to the ship for the price of his first month's wages which the captain would then deduct from his earnings. Not every boarding master was crooked, but the system was open to all sorts of abuse. Many a green youth from the country who put his head in the wrong door on the waterfront had to find his sea legs quickly when he recovered his senses with no land in sight and an angry mate threatening him with brass knuckles.

Despite some notorious cases of brutality against seamen, harsh treatment was more often stupid than intentional. Yankee ships were known for it. They were run to a high standard and demanded work seven days a week. Food was tasty and plentiful; there was no liquor, though molasses-sweetened coffee was provided day and night. But wages in Yankee ships were so low that they attracted only wild

Sore knees, sore hands, sore backs, cold water—deck-scrubbing for apprentices in Illawarra.

characters known as "packet rats." They were tramps, destitutes, and drunkards: "men fit only to keep bread from moulderin'." When a ship was bound for Cape Horn and the sails were slatting themselves to pieces, mates got things done by sheer force of will; they were not the most patient of men.

British ships, known as "lime juicers" because synthetic lime juice was dispensed after twelve days to prevent scurvy, were better manned though living conditions were worse. Owners would spend the absolute minimum on the welfare of their men, though it took no more than a few fresh onions to give a ship a reputation for good living. Staple foods remained the same as long as sailing ships lasted: "salt junk" (beef or pork carried in barrels, often years old) and hardtack (weevily biscuits). The rules gave a man one-and-a-quarter pounds of salt junk a day. The pork might be so fat your thumb sank in it, the beef so hard you could carve ornamental boxes from it. The cook's reputation hung on his "duff," or boiled bread. Flour, bits of grease, and hop yeast were poured into a bag, which was loosely tied at the neck and plunged into a boiling copper for some four hours. Molasses was added later.

It was a rough-and-ready life in sailing ships but it had rewards that could not be obtained ashore, not least of them the sheer joy of spooning through the trades, everything hoisted but the captain's nightshirt, and a hot sun on your back. Men liked the cleanliness of it all, and the peacefulness.

The sea was a hard road but it made tough, dependable, resilient characters. There was certainly no point in getting ill, as one deck boy found in the *Cutty Sark*. When the lad reported sick the captain offered to give him a good clean-out with a wire brush: "I'll reeve the forepart down your throat and the doctor will haul the afterpart out through your stern. Come here now, it's going to do you the world of good..."

RIGHT: *Washing day for a cadet in* Sagres II: *finding the time and opportunity in a crowded ship for these make-and-mend tasks is always a problem.*

FOLLOWING PAGES: *A foreign port after a hard voyage: cadets wave from the fo'c'sle head as Chile's four-masted barquentine* Esmeralda *enters Norfolk, Virginia.*

LIFE ON BOARD

LEFT: *Shaking out cobwebs while* Dar Mlodziezy *is in port, cadets are required to climb to the top of the masts before breakfast.*

RIGHT: *Putting their weight behind the capstan bars, cadets in* Sagres II *haul up the anchor.*

Aboard ship, there is little time for anything but work. Even in this age of radar and satellite navigation, holystones and elbow grease (above) are still employed to keep Gorch Fock II's *decks and gratings smooth and immaculate. Their work done, cadets catch a few moments of peace (right) before their hammocks are stowed to make room for a busy program of classes. In most ships, hammocks have been replaced by bunks.*

LEFT: *Mixed crews are not unusual under sail: these girls are loading supplies aboard* Christian Radich, *of Norway.*

BELOW: *Rude awakening in Gorch Fock: at 6 A.M., cadets parade with rolled-up hammocks to receive orders for the day.*

RIGHT: *Under sail in the Atlantic, in*
Libertad *it is pizza for dinner while the*
radio wedged in the porthole catches news
of World Cup soccer.

A tremble in every knot, stitch, and splice of her, Dar Mlodziezy (right) surges through heavy seas on a bright day in the North Atlantic. For the Polish cadets (above), voyaging under sail has everything to do with sweat, cold, fear, and bloody blisters, and with the intensely per-sonal business of being put through the wringer. There is no hanging back when work is to be done. They do the job, put some polish on it, and by this alone are judged and trusted. Then exhausted after a night of storms, they snatch some sleep with lifelines firmly attached.

LEFT: *A high standard of military-style professionalism is demanded in most of the larger Tall Ships. Captain Ernst Cummings prepares to take the salute during a parade in the* Eagle.

ABOVE: *The largest sailing vessel still afloat is the Soviet Union's* Sedov, *seen here off the English coast. Built in Germany in 1921, the four-masted barque was recently given an extensive refit and now trains fishery cadets.*

ABOVE: *Under full sail, Gorch Fock II of West Germany plows a lonely furrow in the North Sea.*

RIGHT: *Setting sail in* Dar Mlodziezy: *every man has a job to do. It is the responsibility of safety officers to stand back and watch for things likely to go wrong.*

LEFT: *A light breeze on her stern and a small bow wave, her anchors ready to let go and lookouts keeping a sharp eye ahead, the Norwegian full-rigged ship* Christian Radich *makes a landfall with her young crew.*

ABOVE: *A lookout at his lonely post in the bow scans the horizon for shipping as the Portuguese Navy's barque* Sagres II *enters the Gulf of St. Lawrence, bound for Quebec.*

FOLLOWING PAGES: *The perfect peace of a midocean sunset lights up the swelling sails of the* Dar Mlodziezy. *The ship bears this name, which means "gift of youth," because she was paid for by the children of Poland; shipbuilders constructed her in their free time.*

ABOVE: *A spell on the wheel during a dawn watch in the U.S. Coast Guard barque* Eagle; *when maneuvering or sailing in heavy weather, as many as six people are required to handle the wheel.*

RIGHT: *For those off watch, it is "All hands to breakfast!" In the* Eagle *it's scrambled eggs.*

SAIL PLAN

ONE OF FIVE sisters, all virtually identical, the U.S. Coast Guard barque *Eagle* rounds Cape Cod and sets course for her home base at New London, Connecticut.

Four barques, built in Germany during the 1930s for training naval officers, were dispersed to other fleets after the Second World War. Now they are the *Eagle*, flagship of the U.S. Coast Guard, *Sagres II* of the Portuguese Navy, *Tovarisch* of the Soviet Navy, and *Mircea* of Romania. Built from the same plans in

1956, West Germany's *Gorch Fock II* is the fifth of the sisters.

The 1,816-ton *Eagle* is 295 feet long from the delicately shaped counter at her stern to the tip of her bowsprit. Foremast and main mast soar to 147 feet above the water. She has a 728-horsepower diesel engine. Her 22 sails have a total area of 21,530 square feet, are controlled by about 170 different lines, and drive her at a speed that sometimes tops 17 knots (20 miles per hour).

Sail Plan

A Flying jib
B Outer jib
C Inner jib
D Fore topmast staysail
E Fore royal
F Fore topgallant
G Fore upper topsail
H Fore lower topsail

I Foresail
J Main royal staysail
K Main topgallant staysail
L Main topmast staysail
M Main royal
N Main topgallant
O Main upper topsail
P Main lower topsail

Q Mainsail
R Mizzen topgallant staysail
S Mizzen topmast staysail
T Mizzen staysail
U Gaff topsail
V Spanker

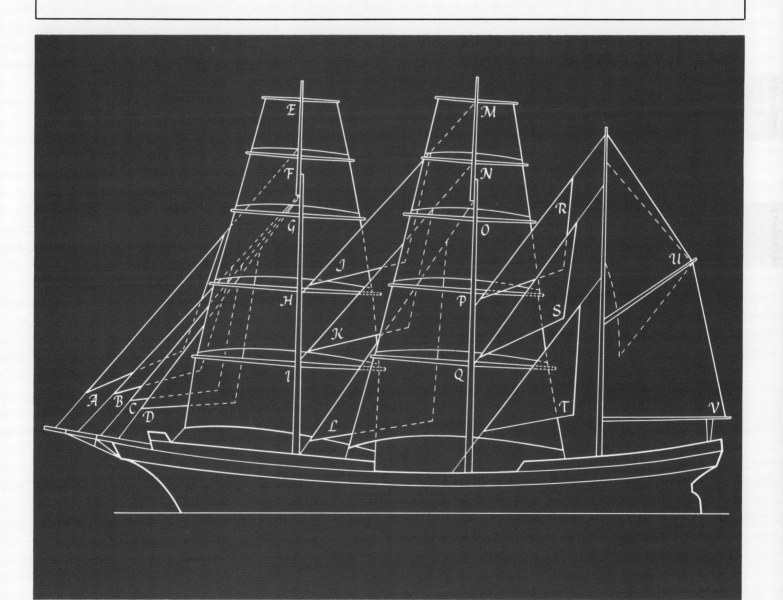

PARADE OF SAIL

THE LONG LINES of visitors queuing patiently on the dockside have disappeared. The vessels have lowered the flags in which they dress for parties. Awnings are unlashed and stowed below. Cadets exchange their crisp shoregoing uniforms for more workmanlike rig. Gangways are hoisted on board. Mooring lines are singled up. Then comes the high point — the parade of sail.

One by one the beautiful ships spread white wings to the wind and head for the far horizon where the chart shows nothing but miles of open ocean ahead. The spectacle of a whole fleet of square-rigged vessels on the move is second to none.

But it is not long before the cheering crowds are left behind, the last TV helicopter turns for home, and the sail-training vessels are alone in their element, where few are fortunate enough to observe them.

BELOW: The figurehead of Sir Winston Churchill *of Great Britain.*

RIGHT: Huge numbers of spectator boats cruise among the sail-training vessels that delight the crowds in Amsterdam.

LEFT: *Figurehead of* Esmeralda *of Chile.*

BELOW: *What better ambassador for a nation than a beautiful sail-powered vessel crewed by young men and women? Eagle shows off her giant colors, and cadets man the rigging as the U.S. Coast Guard barque parades into the port of Mobile, Alabama.*

RIGHT: *Red-shirted cadets man the yards and sing patriotic songs as the Colombian barque* Gloria *leaves her berth in Sydney, Nova Scotia.*

Topsides painted in black and white bands like an old man-of-war, Amerigo Vespucci *(above and top left)* of Italy sets fore-and-aft sails as tugs escort her seaward from the port of Amsterdam.

One of the newest of the Tall Ships, the Mexican naval barque Cuauhtemoc, *(below left)* shows off for New Yorkers during the 1986 parade of sail.

BELOW: With yard and rigging manned, the Dutch schooner Eendracht *joins the parade of sail at Chatham, England.*

RIGHT: *Sails hanging in their gear ready to be stretched to the wind, her cadets manning the yards in traditional gaucho outfits,* Libertad *of Argentina leads a parade of sail-training vessels along the North Sea Canal, Amsterdam.*

3 *Spirit of Cape Horn*

Cape Horn, that tramples beauty into wreck,
And crumples steel and smites the strong man drunk.
JOHN MASEFIELD

FEW SAILORS who glimpsed the massive fist of rock jutting into the gray foam were left in any doubt that the Horn was the greatest of capes. Its sea-ravaged cliffs, plunging from a height of fourteen hundred feet, marked the point where the mountain spine of South America finally dipped beneath the ocean. It was hard to imagine a more suitable finish to a great continent, even harder to find a landmark more dreaded by wind-and-canvas seafarers.

For ships linking the opposite coasts of the Americas, Cape Horn was the only road. In the trade between Australia or New Zealand and their mother country, ships sought the powerful westerly winds and shorter distances of the bleak southern ocean, tracking along the latitudes known as the "roaring forties" until Cape Horn barred the way. The cape forced ships even farther southward, where winds and waves funneled through the narrow gap between continents. This was the Horn, the province of the world's last great commercial sailing ships.

From the opening of the Suez Canal in 1869, steamers ran the beautiful clippers out of the world's prime sea routes and creamed off the cleanest and most remunerative trades. Steamships could run to schedules, like trains, and they were reliable and rapid. The extinction of sail was a certainty, but it would be half a century in the dying; for another generation, sail would continue to evolve.

The figurehead of Cuauhtemoc, *Mexico.*

CRAIGERNE

ROUNDING CAPE HORN

Water in the lee scuppers as the four-masted barque Craigerne, *built 1889, fights round the Horn.*

Sailing ships were relegated to the low-rate cargoes nobody wanted and to the routes that steamers did not have the endurance to handle. Slim profits, bulk cargoes, and long passages were the market forces that shaped the new breed of sailing ship. The speed and daintiness of the tea clipper gave way to a capacious, muscular, and brutish kind of ship.

In the 1830s the typical ocean-going trader had carried about two hundred tons of cargo, the tea clipper of the 1860s about six hundred tons, but the new iron ships built in great numbers through the 1870s and 1880s, mainly in English and Scottish yards, carried well over two thousand tons. The last boom in sail started in 1888. In the next five years, scores of huge sailing ships capable of carrying more than four thousand tons of cargo were sent afloat. Massive and boxy vessels like floating warehouses, they came to be known as windjammers.

For its size, the windjammer may not have attained the marvels of speed that daring captains coaxed out of the flying clippers, though it came close. Besides, the windjammer not only hefted a much bigger load but spread double the amount of canvas on her mighty masts and spars. She made long hauls across the loneliest of oceans with less than half the manpower of a clipper. Typically, a windjammer sailed with a crew of no more than twenty "men" (seamen) and "boys" (green hands). Boys is what they were, for the average age was about eighteen.

Most of the windjammers were four-masted barques, with a handful of five-posters later sailing under French, German, and Scandinavian flags.

One of the last great ports of commercial sail was Newcastle, Australia, where scores of square-riggers await cargo.

Unlike the clippers, windjammers had too few hands to play with fancy sails; nor were sails reefed down. The sails were spread to the wind until the wind was too much, then they were taken in. One spar weighed up to five tons. Steam winches, called "donkey engines," helped with the heaviest work but furling a single sail could be a job for all hands.

Windjammers carried the cargoes for which the world was in no hurry, especially coal to fuel the steamships. Typically, their cavernous holds of sweating steel were filled with coal from Europe outward to Australia or the coasts of Chile and Peru, returning with grain or nitrate fertilizer. Seldom did they dock in comfortable ports. They loaded from lighters far out in the sweltering roads of small Australian railhead ports; in Chilean ports, they anchored in crowded tiers in the open sea off the beaches of godforsaken guano diggings where there was not even a supply of fresh water. Windjammers also carried grain and lumber on the long haul between North America's eastern seaboard and the Pacific northwest and plied other bulk-cargo trades.

By sheer force of geography, for the windjammer most highways led to the dreaded cape of storms — Cape Horn. There was nothing new about the rigors of Old Stiff, as sailors used to call the cape. It had been the fear and dread of seafarers ever since the explorer William Schouten discovered it in 1616 and named it after Hoorn, his birthplace in the Netherlands. The Yankee clippers had beaten their way around the Horn into the teeth of the prevailing westerly weather on their remarkable outward passages to California. Then, running home around the Horn, they had fallen in with the wool clippers heading for Great Britain and Europe from Australia and New Zealand. For the simple reason that it was bigger and its crew smaller, the windjammer brought a new dimension of ferocity and challenge to the war with Cape Horn.

Nowhere else in the world did a ship encounter such spectacular and gigantic seas, commonly half a mile between crests and capped with breaking surf-lines of boiling foam. Whipped across the vast fetches of the southern Pacific and Indian oceans, surging into the bottleneck of the Horn, the daunting waves — commonly as high as a seven-story building — were longer and higher by far than any seen in the North Atlantic. Every danger known to mariners abounded off the Horn. The coasts of Argentina and Chile, converging in an archipelago of flooded alp-like peaks, were an uncivilized and virtually uninhabited wilderness. They offered no sanctuary for a ship to hide from Cape Horn gales and its gigantic graybeard waves, no haven in which to lick wounds and repair damage. There were no beacons or lighthouses to mark the limits of the land.

The gaunt, iron-bound shores were assailed by blizzards, hail squalls, treacherous tides, icebergs, and gale-force fogs. The seawater crashing over the rail of a ship and swirling waist-high along the deck had the temperature of melting ice. The air was at best only fifty degrees Fahrenheit and snow was common in summer. Winds blew at gale force or harder three weeks in four. Most feared of all was the Cape Horn snorter, a squall striking with such fury that water was lifted out of the sea and turned to smoke.

The Horn could also kill a ship with calm weather. When the wind dropped suddenly a ship could rock so violently on the high and greasy swell that the sticks would snap right out of her. If a current carried her close into the manacle rocks along the coast, she was instantly engulfed, with no hope.

At the turn of the century on any one day as many as thirty sailing ships might be fighting their solitary battles against Cape Horn. Half would be reduced to storm canvas, either hove-to or grimly thrashing southward in an effort to win ground against the gales and fight their way out of the Atlantic into the Pacific. Others would be surging eastward with the wind at their backs, crowding on sail to keep up speed and lessen the likelihood of being inundated by a great sea sweeping inboard over the poop. In the immensity of sea and spray, these ships seldom saw each other. When they did, the sight was memorable. An apprentice on the *Springburn* described the spectacle:

It was about noon when she came into view out on our starboard beam.... Flying six topsails, a reefed foresail and a big main top-gallant, she seemed to be daring the savage hail-laden blasts to take the sticks out of her....
It was thrilling to watch the mountains of water chase the ship, just falling short of pooping her, then suddenly divide and rush alongside, gaining in height and bulk until momentum was exhausted. As the sea ran past her, down would go her stem into an abyss from which

Grandest lady of sail: the mighty Preussen, *built in 1902, was the only full-rigged ship with five masts.*

one thought she would never emerge. Up to the heavens raked her jibboom, and her forefoot and keel showed clear almost aft to the foremast.

No ship approached southern latitudes without her rigging overhauled, spars and boats double-lashed, hatches rebattened down, skylights weather-boarded, steering gear overhauled, and lifelines stretched along the maindeck. These preparations were a pleasing ritual of the Cape Horn life. As well, all sails were changed, from the patched and second-rate suit used in light weather to the newest, stoutest sails in her lockers. The men, too, overhauled their Cape Horn rig, patching their oilskins and giving them another lick of linseed oil.

The doubling of Cape Horn was not a simple matter of working around the headland at the southern tip of the Americas' last island. It was a fight to win ground and to survive for the whole distance from fifty degrees south latitude on one side of the continent to fifty degrees south on the other. Ruled off the chart in straight lines, this made a distance of about thirteen hundred sea miles; a well-driven ship might sail it in as little as six days. Given a lucky break in the weather and indomitable nerve, a six-day turn could be achieved even when sailing from the Atlantic to the Pacific into the teeth of the prevailing westerlies. But the Horn was not noted for lucky breaks. From fifty degrees south, a ship was in a battle that could last days or weeks or months.

The lazy way to round the Horn was to head-reach under fore topsails, virtually hove-to like a seabird with its head tucked into its wing, until the winds turned favorable. But you could wait a long time for fair winds off the cape of storms. Some ships took such a battering that they turned tail and ran with the westerlies, heading the other way and going right around the globe to reach their destination.

Yet Captain Robert Helgendorf, known as "the devil of Hamburg" for his hard-driving passages, rounded the Horn sixty-six times as master of

Germany's Laeisz "Flying P" ships. In twenty years of command, Helgendorf never took more than ten days to fight one of his heavily laden ships around the Horn. It took tramp steamers another quarter century to improve on his average.

In Helgendorf's view, no ship ought to make an easy passage by heaving-to and waiting. He would hoist every sail his ship could stagger under, then thrash southward. Holding on to a press of sail prevented the westerly gales from driving the ship to leeward. He would storm across the gale, down to the icy latitudes of sixty degrees south if he had to, and only then head northward on the other tack. By then the land would be weathered, and after ten days the Horn was well astern.

Among the most successful of the sailing-ship lines, the Flying P line started in the nitrate trade in the 1850s. By the end of the century, it was running a fleet of Cape Horners whose names have gone down in the history of sail as the noblest of the breed. Not one was dismasted or overwhelmed; not one turned tail on the Horn. Even their royals, the highest and smallest of the sails, were sewn from double-strength Cape Horn canvas.

Mightiest of them all was the *Preussen*, 408 feet long, and the only full-rigged (with square rig on every mast) five-poster. Built in 1902, she matched the tramp steamer ton for ton, man for man, and knot for knot, yet her owners paid no bills for machinery or fuel. Most of her crew slaved at her heavy rigging for a pittance, only because they loved to sail. But it was a steamer, misjudging her speed, that ran her down in the Dover Strait in 1910.

Many a windjammer suffered a similar fate because sailing ships were not required to carry lights at the masthead. When spray was flying, it took a sharp-eyed lookout on the bridge of a steamer to spot a dim red or green navigation light.

Fewer sailing ships were built after the turn of the century, yet despite the best efforts of steamers to run them down they were a long time dying out. Some three hundred square-riggers still flew the Red Ensign in 1910, though they were fast being sold abroad, and submarines and raiders in the First World War would soon spell the end of deep water sail under the British flag. The racing tradition, however, remained a strong one. When ship met ship on the high seas, neither captain cared to be outdistanced; both captains would crack on all sail.

Though windjammers steadily lost ground to steamships on the open ocean, small sailing ships built locally of wood were still very much the workhorses of the coasts. Their size was no deterrent to prodigious voyages. Many of these able, seaworthy, and graceful little sailing vessels, though no more than a hundred tons, sailed on sealing voyages to the remotest parts of the world and regularly crossed the Atlantic. Every coast had its family of doughty holding their own against the onslaught of steamships, motor trucks, and railways. The sailor's eye could instantly identify by its lines the bluff-bowed galeas of the Baltic, the shallow sprit-sail barge of the British coast, the skipjacks and bugeyes of Chesapeake Bay, the yachtlike "Indian-headed" and "sharpshooter" clipper schooners fishing the Grand Banks.

The end of sail. Swept by combers, the Cromdale *ran ashore off The Lizard, Cornwall, during thick fog in 1913.*

Once the damaging Civil War was behind her, the United States looked inland to the exploitation of her great heartland. Her merchant marine never recovered the glory it had enjoyed in clipper days, but the shipwrights of New England and the Maritimes of Canada persevered with construction in timber, the one material they had in abundance. From slipways in bays and inlets along the entire seaboard, they turned out the last word in a distinctive type of vessel called the schooner.

By 1897 about fourteen hundred iron and composite sailing ships flew the British flag, compared with only eighty under the Stars and Stripes. But the United States fielded more than two thousand trading schooners, three times more than Great Britain. It was said that in every schooner sailed a little of the heart of every man in the town that built her. The schooners were the workhorses of the coast and held out longest against mechanical power because they were cheap to build and required few men to sail. In remote areas such as the outports of Newfoundland and the Pacific Islands, sailing schooners with auxiliary engines remained a primary means of transport up to the 1950s.

Among the American schooner fleet were large vessels that could carry as much cargo as windjammers. They were the "down easters": fast, capacious, and weatherly ships that beat around the Horn to load grain in California and Puget Sound. Some ran across the Atlantic to Europe with cargoes of lumber. They hoisted huge fore-and-aft gaff sails on each of their five masts, voyaged so heavily laden that their decks were awash, and counted their crew in terms of one man per mast, plus a master, a mate, and a cook. Their decline began with the opening of transcontinental railroads; the final blow was dealt by the opening of the Panama Canal in 1914.

At the turn of the century, Britain began to discard her Cape Horners. France, on the other hand, instituted high subsidies for building new ones and paid a bounty for every sea mile logged under sail. No fewer than a hundred and fifty big steel four-masters were built in eight years, and France had by far the biggest windjammer fleet in the world. Her pride was the *France*, a five-masted barque sunk in 1901 when a British warship plowed into her while she was at anchor. The *France II*, built twelve years later for the ore trade with New Caledonia, was the largest sailing vessel ever built. The gigantic rig of the 419-foot five-masted barque was said to have thirty-eight miles of rigging. She drifted on a coral reef in 1922.

When the subsidies stopped, just before the First World War, so did the ships. French ports were crammed with first-class idle windjammers. Many were later sunk by enemy action, mainly by submarine crews who didn't waste a torpedo but scuttled them with time bombs. By 1928 France's last square-rigger was out of commission; in 1929 Britain's last Cape Horner, the *Garthpool*, drifted ashore on Cape Verde in a calm. In America, a few old full-riggers and barques were kept on to sail every spring from San Francisco to Alaska with men and fish-canning equipment. But this packing fleet steadily declined as vessels were lost at sea, run aground, burned out, sold to Hollywood, or anchored off Long Beach as gaming palaces. By 1939 only one was fit for sea.

Through the 1920s, Hamburg and Antwerp were the last true sailing-ship ports in Europe and enough trade was carried under sail for Germany to insist that a man could not be granted a second-mate's certificate without serving his time before the mast. But the rule had to be changed through lack of ships in 1929, three years after the launching of *Padua*, the last big square-rigged merchant vessel to be built.

Sailing ships enjoyed one last surge of glory between the wars. From his base in Mariehamn, in the Aland Islands of Finland, Gustav Erikson rescued the last of the windjammers from the scrap heap, buying them at knockdown prices and sailing them without insurance. His fleet of fifteen Cape Horners and about twenty other sailing ships was operated on a shoestring.

Few commercial voyages were made under sail after the Second World War. The last honest-to-God Cape Horners to continue trading were the *Pamir* and the *Passat*, bought from the knacker's yard by a Hamburg owner and fitted with big diesel engines. Most voyaging was done under power and the big four-masted barques never paid their way. Homeward bound from Buenos Aires in 1957, the *Pamir* three times rolled her yardarms into the sea, then turned turtle and never came up. Her cargo of barley, loaded loose instead of in sacks, flowed like liquid as she rolled, and it held her down. Only six of her eighty-six crew members were rescued. It was the end of the great Cape Horners in commercial sail.

Today, two great windjammers continue to spread their wings to the wind as training ships for the Fisheries Ministry of the Soviet Union: *Kruzenshtern* (ex *Padua*) and the *Sedov* (ex *Magdalene Vinnen*). Others slumber with folded wings as museum ships: *Peking* and *Wavertree* at South Street, Manhattan; *Balclutha* at Fishermen's Wharf in San Francisco; *Elissa* in Galveston; *Falls of Clyde* in Honolulu; *Moshulu* in Philadelphia; *Star of India* in San Diego; *Pommern* in Mariehamn; *Passat* in Travemunde; and *Seute Deern* in Bremerhaven.

Windjammers no longer trample down the Cape Horn road, but the spirit of that dreaded cape endures.

4 Aloft and Stow!

Growl you may but go you must.
SAILORS' MAXIM

HE SUNRISE is wild and grand. Gray and sickly green, the seas run in long, foam-flecked ridges. Thundering graybeards rise above these rolling hills, look around for a victim, then subside with a hiss and a roar. The ship rolls heavily in a mass of white froth, scooping green water over her bulwarks. Waves surge knee-deep across the deck and fill the scuppers.

In the fo'c'sle, sea chests and gear swirl in the tide of water that slops back and forth, reaching as high as the upper bunks. Wrapped in a wet blanket in a wet bunk, you sleep in your boots. They are squelchy despite the newspaper wrapped around your feet. Precious matches were wasted lighting paper in a fruitless attempt to dry and warm them. Then a voice with all the power of the gale behind it bursts with a spray of water over the storm sill: "All hands! All hands! Out on deck, yer pussycats!"

The rain tastes of salt as you stumble out into the disheveled wilderness. The hard, cold wind penetrates every crevice of thin oilskins, despite extra layers around the waist, wrists, and ankles. Icicles hang from the deckhouse but the two men on the wheel are sweating. Desperately, they work to prevent the ship from broaching sideways to the giant seas racing up astern. The ship's wake is a jagged line reaching like a crack in a cliff up the face of the looming wave. The helmsmen do not look over their shoulders lest they lose their nerve. But somehow the shimmering gray wall of water seems to stoop. Tucking its shoulders around the ship's stern, it tosses her forward in a wild, roaring, surging ride.

Aloft, every wire and rope is an iron bar humming, whining, shrieking, fluting different notes. Big as barn roofs, the bulging sails are as hard and gray as slate. The royals on the highest yards have not been set for a week; nor have the great courses on the lowest yards. All the drive is in the upper and lower topgallants and the upper and lower topsails, four racks of canvas on each mast. The Old Man has decided the power of the gale is too great. The topgallants must come off.

No time now for romantic notions about the glory of sail. This is the wind and weather for nerve, balance, strength, and guts. It is a job for seamen....

Aloft in the rigging of a sailing ship, a seaman was in his element. (And, it was said, as near to heaven as he would ever get.) The dizzy heights and wildly exaggerated motion of the ship's swoop and roll held no terrors. He was brought up to it. He knew every inch of the great web of rigging stretched among the masts and spars and could clamber around it as confidently as he trod the cobblestones of home. In a three-masted ship, nearly three hundred adjustable ropes came down from aloft and were cleated to stout pegs called belaying pins. The seaman could locate any of them instantly by touch.

Developed and refined by practical seafarers over centuries, the rigging of sailing ships had few variations, and the pattern for every mast was much the same. Every rope and block served a purpose, every coil had its place. The rig of a sailing ship was the epitome of order and function.

A ship had two kinds of rigging. The standing rigging, which stayed the masts and transmitted the power of the sails to the hull, was permanent. It included the heavy shrouds which stopped the masts from falling sideways and came down to the rails of the ship; the shrouds were fitted with horizontal ropes, called ratlines, which provided a ladder for the crew to go aloft.

The running rigging was the complex system of adjustable chains, wires, and ropes by which the sails were set and trimmed to the wind. When working aloft it was unwise to use the running rigging for handholds because it could suddenly run out or flail in the wind.

The square sails were hung from horizontal spars called yards. When making sail, the canvas on half of them was pulled down or simply let drop. The yards of the others were hoisted from the deck, thereby stretching the sails upward. Ropes from the sides and from the bottom corners of each sail stretched the canvas across the wind to trap its power. The ropes passing around the sail hauled it up to the yard, muzzling it before the men went aloft to gather it in and lash it down.

On every mast the entire trembling edifice of canvas was rotated by hauling on long ropes called braces. Like bridles, these led to the ends of each yard and came down to massive belaying pins on each side of the deck. When the ship rolled, the pins were often dipped underwater.

The gaps between the masts had two or three triangular fore-and-aft sails called staysails. Other staysails were hoisted on the headstays, which came down to the bowsprit; a big gaff sail called a driver or spanker was hoisted on the aft side of the mizzen.

On cold southern seas in 1912, oilskinned crewmen make running repairs to the rigging of Terra Nova.

Cold water spills dangerously over the bulwarks as Garthsnaid *battles through a storm; in these conditions it was safer for a man to be aloft than on deck.*

In merchant sailing ships, crews were small and teamwork was the byword. Every man pulled more than his weight. No room at sea for slackers or the faint-hearted, especially aloft in wild weather.

To go aloft, a sailor climbed the weather side of the rigging so the wind flattened him against the ratlines instead of blowing him off. The rule was to cut through any ratline showing signs of rot; rotten lines would break under a man's weight. When it was "Aloft and stow!" in a ship scudding before a storm in southerly latitudes, there was work to be done. The sailor who could not hang on with eyebrows and belly muscles, leaving two hands free, was not up to the job.

The fight with canvas was the ultimate test of a sailor. First that climb up the thrumming rigging to a yard slanting perilously over a seething, frigid ocean. Then the unhesitating step from the ratlines to a slender footrope slung beneath the spar. It juddered as the festoons of flapping canvas cracked the air like artillery fire. The footrope sagged under your weight, so the yard came level with your chin, but tightened as more men put their weight on it. A long-legged sailor often found the footropes so short he had to kneel on the yard.

The sail was first muzzled from the deck, the clewlines being hauled, to bring up the corners of the sail and the buntlines gathering the belly of the sail up to the yard. Then you leaned over the yard, reaching far down over it to grab a fold of wind-rattled canvas. Hauling it up, you wedged a good bunch of it under your belly then grabbed some more. When all the sail lay on top of the spar it was beaten down with fists then rolled into its own skin and lashed down.

Sounds simple. But the canvas was stiff as a board, sodden with icy water, and flogging heavily in the gale. You were clinging to a wildly gyrating stick as high as seventeen stories above the deck. It was a single-handed struggle with something much greater than yourself, said Joseph Conrad. Yet, as John Masefield testified in his *Being Ashore*, men derived from the struggle a unique satisfaction:

> My royal was the mizzen royal, a rag of a sail among the clouds, a great grey rag, leaping and slatting 160 feet above me. The wind beat me down against the shrouds, it banged me and blew the tears from my eyes. It seemed to lift me up the futtocks into the top, and up the topmast rigging to the crosstrees. In the crosstrees I learned what wind was....
>
> I lay out on the yard, and the sail hit me in the face and knocked my cap away. It beat me and banged me, and blew from my hands. The wind pinned me flat against the yard, and seemed to be blowing all my clothes to shreds. I felt like a king, like an emperor. I shouted aloud with the joy of that "rastle" with the sail.

Heavy and gray, chill and damp were the days that came and went while a ship pounded her easting down, running across southern latitudes toward Cape Horn. Strangely, compared with the oblivion and soft tranquility of trade-wind sailing in the tropics, men found it an experience of soaring exultation. Just wind and sea and rigging and fighting canvas. But what a fight!

Wrapped in spume and wind, the *Herzogin Cecilie* ran for Cape Horn in 1928. For thirty-six straight hours, all hands toiled to reduce sail. Then the weather sheet of the *Cecilie's* fore upper staysail was carried away. Alan Villiers tells the story.

> We learned that so far we had been only playing, for when we tried to clew that upper topsail up before we lay aloft, every bit of its gear carried away except the lee clewline. We stared up in dismay, though we could see nothing. We were pretty far gone then, and tired, and worn out.
>
> "Aloft and furl it," said the mate and led the way himself. We followed, and the morning broke before we came down again.
>
> It looked madness to go on that yard and maybe it was. It looked madness to try to reach it and maybe it was. But we went just the same....
>
> The whole foremast was shaking and quivering with the furious thrashing of the sail; the great steel yard quivered and bent; the rigging shook violently as if it wanted to shake us off into the sea boiling beneath. The loose ends of the broken sheet and the wire

buntlines were flying around through the air, writhing like steel and chain snakes; if any of us had been touched by these it would have been the end....

I have not the faintest idea how we got that sail fast. I don't think anyone who was there has. We fought it times without number, and lost; but there came a time when we fought it and won. But that was not before our bare hands — you cannot fight wet canvas with gloves — were red with blood and blue with cold.

A flying buntline touched one of the German seamen in the head once, and brought swift blood. He reeled a bit, but carried on. Then he fainted, after a while, and because we could not take him down we had to lash him there. When he revived he carried on again.

One able seaman's struggle to reef an upper topsail, recounted by Basil Lubbock in *The Last of the Windjammers*, ended less happily:

There were twenty-four men up on that yard, a dozen on either yardarm. As the sail was loosed the wind broke into it and a huge white balloon swelled up as hard as an iron shell.

We might as well have tried to gather in the wind itself. The skipper on the poop saw how impossible was our task so he ordered the man at the wheel to luff a trifle, that the strength of the wind might be taken out of the sail's belly.

The cook was at the wheel and he was not an experienced seaman. It was too late when the skipper himself snatched the revolving spokes.

The white mass gave a quiver, began to shiver; then bang, bang, bang, it thundered and flapped, rolled up and down, smothered over the line of clinging men, pressing them to the yard and shaking the mast itself with mighty jerks.

Just then one of the clews carried away, releasing the sail from the yardarm below. The heavy clew-iron and leech swished about like a whip, striking among the backstays and rigging.

I heard a shriek, even above all this noise. A shower of drops flew past my eyes and splattered the canvas red. The man next to me was bleeding about the head: his sou'wester was gone and his hair was shining red. Some irresistible influence caused me to look down. Before our fo'c'sle door lay a figure in yellow oilskins, splotched with dark stains.

Finally there came a momentary lull in the gale wind and, after an hour's struggle, we did at last reef the sail. From end to end the yard was covered in red hand prints.

For all its hardship and danger, fighting sails high in the rigging of a Cape Horner was generally less hazardous than hauling on the braces and other gear belayed on her maindeck. While the clipper had a sea-kindly shape and inherent buoyancy in her timbers, there was nothing kindly or buoyant about the massive, square-cut hull of a rust-streaked windjammer driving hard through a storm. When loaded, freeboard was barely four-and-a-half feet, little enough when thrashing

The crew of the three-masted ship Torrens was lucky to be alive after a head-on collision with an iceberg during a voyage to Adelaide in 1899.

through rolling black and gray hills half as high as the masthead. The clipper had been cursed for her wetness when cutting through head seas, but the spray obliterating her deck was nothing to the solid tons of green water rolling over the low bulwarks of a hard-pressed four-poster.

No man could resist the power of a killer wave crashing aboard like a cartload of bricks. He could leap for a lifeline, make himself small, hang on like grim death, hold his breath. But once his grip was loosened the raging water carried him willy-nilly. Many men were carried helplessly overboard. There was hardly any point in throwing a lifebuoy, for it would only prolong the luckless man's agony: the ship could never be turned around, a boat could never be launched. But many a sailor carried over the side by one wave found himself miraculously dumped on board again by the next.

A good captain made the best use of a gale blowing in the right direction, hanging on to his sails as long as he could. But when his judgment failed the vessel would ship a mighty mass of water over the poop. Frank T. Bullen described such an experience:

> You are running before the wind and waves, sometimes deep in the valley between liquid mountains, sometimes high on the rolling ridge of one. You watch anxiously the speed of the sea, trying to decide whether it or you are going faster, when suddenly there seems to be a hush, almost a lull, in the uproar. You look astern and see a wall of water rising majestically higher and higher, at the same time drawing nearer and nearer. Instinctively you clutch something firm, and hold your breath. Then that mighty green barrier leans forward,

the ship's stern seems to settle at the same time, and, with a thundering noise as of an avalanche descending, it overwhelms you.

The lucky men in the rigging would see the entire deck of the ship covered from rail to rail in ripping water. The force of the wave would smash bulwarks, demolish deckhouses, splinter lifeboats into driftwood. And if the raging sea found the smallest fingerhold beneath the tarpaulins and hatch covers, the ship was dead.

Even if a ship struggled free of the terrible wave, there was a good chance the helmsman had been carried away and the wheel smashed. Then she would broach, swinging broadside to the next great wave. Thrown on her beam ends, wave after wave would break right over her. If the ship were not broken up by the weight and power of falling water as she lay on her side, yardarms piercing the water, there was a grave danger the cargo would shift and prevent her coming upright.

But still a ship could survive, if fate were with her. The rigging was cut away, no easy matter when it was made of iron and steel, and the crew sent with shovels into the cramped and pitch-dark hold which was battened down behind them. Then they dug for their lives, heaving the cargo up to the high side and damming it there with boards, toiling without pause and praying that the next perilous lurch did not drown them like rats in a trap.

And there was the risk of a dismasting. The knock-on effect of one vital piece of standing gear breaking could be calamitous. If the bobstay parted, the bowsprit was left unsupported. This would bring the fore topmast down with a crash, dragging the main topgallant mast after it, and so on.

There was ice. In hard years, the pack ice drifted up to the Horn itself. In late winter and early spring, the ocean south of sixty degrees was at least a quarter pack ice. More dangerous were the "growlers," small chunks of ice not much larger than a piano, which floated awash and invisible but were fatal to a ship that hit one at speed. Many a ship was saved from ice by a man's nose for the dank, bottom-of-the-fridge smell of ice ahead, or by the echo of a foghorn bouncing off an iceberg's cliffs.

Strangely, although the road to the Horn was paved with every imaginable peril and hardship, there was never a shortage of young men and boys to pit their wits and their muscle against it.

Notwithstanding the cold, the discomfort, the wet, the man-killing work in the pitch darkness, and the washing about on the decks, a certain kind of man thoroughly enjoyed it. Why, but for the sake of some inexpressible spirit that moved his soul, the spirit of sail? As Alex Hurst wrote: "The sheer glory of sailing through these waters, under short canvas perhaps, but with all the sensation of being picked up and hurled forwards on our wild way as if by some mad and drunken god, made a man's soul shout for sheer joy at all the wonder within him."

The triumph of a few puny men in wind-rattled oilskins amid a great and disheveled wilderness, the beauty of a ship, glistening with wetness, surging through gigantic seas: this was the spirit of working high canvas in windjammer days.

RIGHT: *Running repairs to* Gorch Fock II *'s main royal staysail: a crew member straddles a headstay high above the sea.*

FOLLOWING PAGES: *With fingers, fists, knees, teeth, and guts, cadets aloft in* Sagres II *tame their sail and lash it tightly to the spar.*

WORKING ALOFT

Setting everything but the captain's night-shirt, the British topsail schooner Malcolm Miller (*above and right*) at the start of the Cutty Sark Tall Ships Race from Newcastle upon Tyne to Bremerhaven. To furl the big square sail, young crew members lay out on the yard then haul the gathered sail up to their bellies and punch it into a neat roll.

LEFT: *For green sailors the most nerve-racking moment when climbing aloft is getting over the futtock shrouds beneath the top (the platform in the lower part of the picture) then swinging up on to the cross-trees. A crew member of* Eagle *shows how it is done.*

ABOVE: *Curtseying over small swells in the Gulf of St. Lawrence, the Colombian Navy's barque* Gloria *heads for Quebec.*

FOLLOWING PAGES: *Work in a sailing ship is never done but has a pleasing simplicity and rhythm: cadets replace a storm-damaged topsail as* Libertad *cruises in the Caribbean.*

Snugging down for the night, cadets (above) furl topsails in Sagres II; *in this Portuguese barque (right), commands are given from the deck by boatswains' whistles.*

FOLLOWING PAGES: *There was no peace in the world except in a sailing ship, old sailors used to say: as* Dar Mlodziezy *ghosts across the Gulf Stream in light winds, a few moments' respite for cadets standing on the ratlines to enjoy the sunset.*

One thing Cape Horn never saw: female crew members. Cadets like this girl (left) furling sail aloft in Eagle are increasingly common in today's Tall Ships and work alongside their male shipmates at all tasks, including swinging on the footropes high above the sea (above) to make a shipshape stow of Eagle's upper topsail as night falls.

ABOVE: *Working aloft was a struggle with something much greater than yourself,* re-*ported the Polish sea captain and English author Joseph Conrad. Here, Polish cadets wrestle with sails in* Dar Mlodziezy.

RIGHT: *The experience of shared dangers and discomforts forges a unique bond among a vessel's crew members: aloft in* Sagres II, *a young Portuguese flattens himself to the spar so a shipmate can pass.*

ABOVE: Cadets on the "tops" of the Gorch Fock II struggle to secure the staysail during strengthening winds.

RIGHT: Polish cadets work aloft in Dar Mlodziezy. To be useful in the rigging requires nerve, agility, and guts. It is work for real sailors.

WORKING SHIP

THE RIG OF a sailing ship is an infinitely adjustable and complex engine. It exists for the sole purpose of harnessing the wind's power to drive the vessel forward. To get the best from it, however, requires skill and artistry. There's no question of setting the sails then sitting back. The ship has to be worked. That is, sails have to be continually trimmed and adjusted to take into account changing conditions of wind and sea.

First, the wind is always changing course and it blows from a significantly different direction the higher you go up the mast. The faster the ship sails, the more the wind direction seems to draw ahead, requiring more adjustments. Second, ropes become slack as the sun soaks moisture out of them, and sails may blanket one another on different points of sailing. These factors can affect the ship's balance, making her heavy to steer and slowing her down because too much rudder action has a braking effect. To keep a ship sailing at her best speed on a steady course therefore demands constant attention, skill, and hard work.

A vessel sails smoothly and easily in the same direction as the wind, and swiftly and steadily across the wind. But it cannot sail directly into the wind's eye. Instead, the best it can do is a series of zigzags, called tacks. At the end of every tack it must turn to bring the wind on the other side.

When the bows are turned into the wind, the vessel is "tacking." This is a complex maneuver requiring slick and concentrated teamwork. A square-rigger is designed for the wind to push her from behind; all her masts and spars are stayed with that in mind. But now the wind will be acting on the forward side of the sails. For a short time the vessel might even make sternway, sailing backward. But if the maneuver is properly executed, the vessel will turn up into the wind, swing her yards around at exactly the right moment, and head off on the other tack with no ground lost.

When winds are either very strong or very light, the vessel might have problems tacking into the wind. Instead, the crew will "wear" or "veer" the ship, bringing the wind to bear on her other side by turning her stern toward it. This method can lose a lot of hard-won distance and requires more sea room than tacking, but is easier with a small crew.

On deck, all seems chaos from the moment the order goes out, "Ready about!" Cadets race to their stations, throw the coiled ropes off the pins, check that they are free to pay out, then sound off: "Foremast manned and ready!"

The watch officer makes sure the vessel has gathered as much speed as possible then gives the order to put the rudder hard over. This is done slowly to prevent loss of speed. The ship shoots up into the wind. Staysails are lowered. The mainsail is hauled up to its yard. Headsails slat noisily as their sheets are shifted to the other side. The spanker boom is hauled amidships.

Tacking Ship

Wearing Ship

Key to Diagrams   *filling*   *lifting*   *backing*

"Mainsail haul!" The sails on the main mast are braced round as soon as they begin to lift. This is a critical moment. If anything gets stuck the ship could be caught "in irons," unable to turn one way or the other while the wind drives her backward, and she is vulnerable to dismasting.

As the sails on the main fill and begin to drive the ship ahead it's "Let go and haul!" The yards on the foremast are quickly braced round and the sails fill. The helmsman spins the wheel amidships then meets her and the ship settles down on her new course. On deck there is hectic activity. The mainsail and staysails are set again. The sails are trimmed, then the many ropes are coiled and hung neatly on their pins. When smartly executed the whole maneuver takes about eight minutes.

PREVIOUS PAGE: *Whistles blowing, boots stamping on the wet deck, cadets in* Gorch Fock II *race to raise topgallants. They run along the deck with one halyard and back with another, so the heavy spars are hoisted smoothly and in unison.*

Keeping his rig tuned to its finest pitch, the whole "engine" driving the ship with maximum power, is the shipmaster's obsession but he has only the brawn and skill of his crew with which to do it. The cadets in Gorch Fock II (*above and right*) *put their backs into it.*

FOLLOWING PAGES: *Bracing round in* Eagle: *heavy yards swivel on the mast as cadets far below, photographed from the main crosstrees, heave on the braces.*

MAN OVERBOARD

"MAN OVERBOARD!" The cry strikes a chill in the heart of every sailor. In the old days of sail, when large vessels were handled by small crews, it was impossible to turn the ship around. Sometimes it was considered merciful not to throw any lifebuoys. In heavy weather a vessel risked her masts if she tried to stop or turn. But this is not the case in modern well-manned training vessels where regular drills are part of the routine.

Under full sail with a strong following wind, near Miami in 1976, a cadet tumbled off the bowsprit of the Norwegian ship *Christian Radich*. So well drilled was the crew that the ship was stopped, a boat launched, and the cadet returned safely on board within twelve minutes.

At the shout of "Man overboard!" alarms sound through the vessel and all hands race on deck. Lifebuoys are thrown, with smoke flares or lights to mark the position. The lifeboat's crew and its launching team make ready. At the same time the ship is stopped by heaving-to, with sails on the main mast thrown "aback" to act as a brake. Main and fore courses are hauled up to their yards; headsails and staysails are lowered and the engine is started. Meanwhile, lookouts keep their eyes fixed on the lost man's position and the lifeboat is directed by radio.

Man Overboard Procedures Under Sail

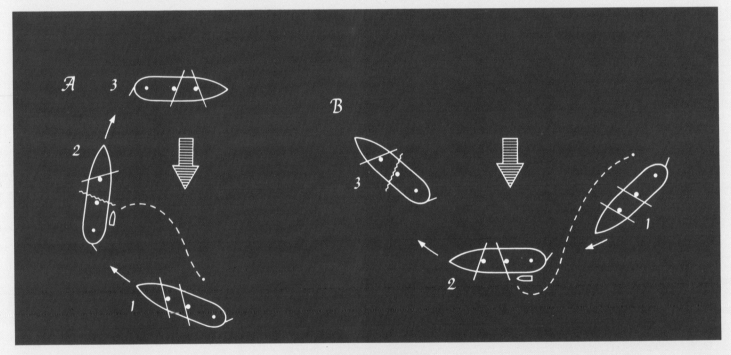

A. On the Wind

1. Right full rudder
2. Lower the boat on lee side
3. Lower fore and aft sails and courses

B. Off the Wind

1. Right full rudder
2. Let go and haul
3. Lower fore and aft sails and courses

LEFT: *Man overboard drills can be exhausting: a Polish Merchant Marine Academy cadet in* Dar Mlodziezy.

BELOW: *Practicing man overboard maneuvers in the North Sea,* Gorch Fock II *is "heaved to," headsails and staysails lowered, main course hauled up, and yards on the main mast set "aback."*

THE RIGS OF SAILING VESSELS

A full-rigged ship is a royal queen,
*   Way-hay for Boston town, oh!*
A lady at court is a barquentine,
A barque is a gal with ringlets fair,
A brig is the same with shorter hair,
A topsail schooner's a racing mare,
*   But a schooner, she's a clown oh!*
*   —Sailormen's Shanty*

IN DAYS OF SAIL when every quayside was a forest of masts and spars, types of sailing vessels were not described by their hulls but by their rigs. Since these are the parts that lift over the horizon first, a distant craft can be identified through a telescope long before her hull is visible. Although there were many variations, rigs became more or less standardized. There are two principal systems of rig: square rig and fore-and-aft rig.

SQUARE RIG The sails are square or rectangular and spread from horizontal spars, called yards, which cross the masts. These sails are designed to be pushed by the wind; the wind always strikes them on the same side (the back). Square sails perform best when sailing across or down the wind. The system allows a big ship to split a vast area of canvas into many small areas so each one is handled by relatively few seamen.

FORE-AND-AFT RIG Sails are attached to masts or to wires by the luff, or leading edge, like those of a modern yacht. They use the wind first on one side then the other, depending on the vessel's course. Not ideal for long passages in following winds but able to drive a vessel at an angle into the teeth of the weather, the fore-and-aft rig was developed mainly in smaller coastal vessels. Square-riggers have a number of fore-and-aft sails to improve windward capability. Many fore-and-aft vessels hoist a square sail or two when running downwind.

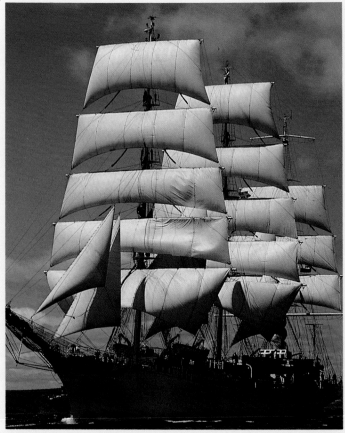

Dar Mlodziezy, *Poland.*

SHIP The full-rigged vessel, or ship, had square sails on all masts. Through the nineteenth century a large number of three-masted ships were built, including the clippers, and they traded in every ocean of the world. About fifty "four-poster" ships were launched after 1870, and in 1902 the great five-master *Preussen* was built.

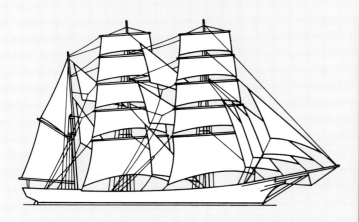

BARQUE Usually with three masts, the barque is square-rigged on all but the aftermost mast, which has a fore-and-aft gaff sail. The barque was very common, and many "ships" were converted into barques because the rig was slightly cheaper and easier to handle. In four-masted barques the after mast was called the jigger.

Elissa, *U.S.A.*

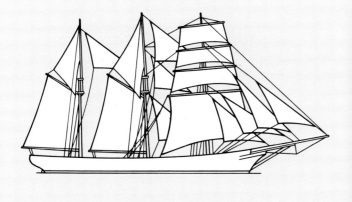

BARQUENTINE The name implies three masts but some were built with as many as six. The rig combines both systems, with large fore-and-aft sails on all masts but the foremast, thus reducing the costs of rigging and manpower.

Juan Sebastian de Elcano, *Spain.*

Royalist, *United Kingdom.*

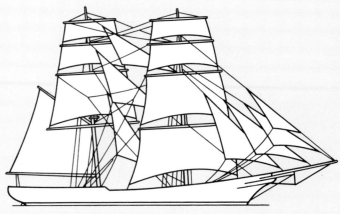

BRIG Found in every corner of the world before the schooner, the brig is square-rigged on each of its two masts with a fore-and-aft sail called a spanker on the main mast.

Asgard II, *Ireland.*

BRIGANTINE With two masts, square-rigged on the foremast and fore-and-aft rigged on the main mast, the brigantine was particularly favored in North America, where it was also known as a "half brig" or "hermaphrodite brig."

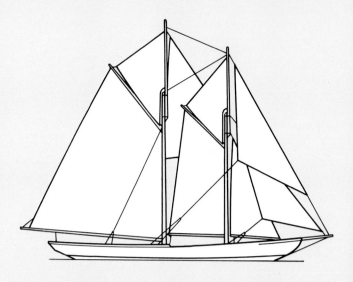

SCHOONER Developed in North America as the workhorse of the east coast, with two or more masts, the schooner seldom carried any square sails. Most were smallish, nimble, weatherly craft but some had seven masts and were among the largest sailing vessels ever built.

Bluenose II, *Canada.*

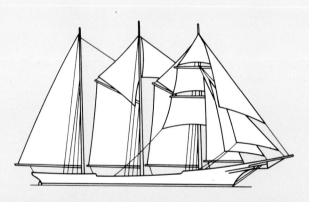

TOPSAIL SCHOONER Mainly a British development of the American schooner, the topsail schooner carried one or two square sails on the upper part of the foremast in addition to fore-and-aft sails. This improved her downwind performance. Most were small but sailed on long, hard voyages. The rig is popular in large modern vessels.

Malcolm Miller, *United Kingdom.*

RIGS OF SMALL VESSELS

KETCH Two masts, the after mast (mizzen) shorter than the main mast and positioned ahead of the rudder post.

YAWL Two masts like a ketch but the mizzen is positioned aft of the rudder post.

CUTTER One mast with more than one headsail.

SLOOP One mast with one headsail.

5 Spirit of Tall Ships

The God that hauled, the keel that sailed, are changed beyond recall,
But the robust and brassbound man, he is not changed at all.
RUDYARD KIPLING

IN THE DAYS of sail a seaman was bred to the sea. He learned the craft of his trade the hard but certain way, by doing. It was a tough and difficult road. The ship's boy, perhaps twelve years old, was at the beck and call of every man on board. The captain might exert some sort of rough guardianship over his welfare, but the captain had traveled the road himself and was not inclined to make it softer for those who followed. But if a boy survived the knocks he could become first a mate and then, at a remarkably young age, the master of a full-rigged ship setting sail for foreign parts.

From the middle of the nineteenth century, legislation to improve the safety and conditions of life at sea was introduced slowly but progressively. Vessels had to carry certain lights. The deliberate overloading of ships was prevented. Crews' rations had to exceed specified amounts. For deck officers, minimum levels of competence were established for each stage of the ladder to promotion. To gain the certificate, or "ticket," entitling him to act as mate or shipmaster, a man proved his fitness by submitting to a written and oral examination. But first he had to serve his time at sea.

In British vessels, and with minor differences in most other merchant fleets, the first stage was an apprenticeship of three years and four months

The British topsail schooner Sir Winston Churchill *racing across the southern North Sea from Chatham in England to Zeebrugge in Belgium. Frequently this three-master is sailed by an all-girl crew.*

before the mast. A boy's family paid a premium, and the boy was formally indentured to a shipowner at the age of fourteen. In return, he was supposed to get sufficient training in seamanship and navigation to be certified as second mate. But anything he learned was his own business. In reality, most owners exploited the system for cheap labor.

Apprentices wore jauntily angled peak caps with their company's flag on its badge. The only badge of rank was the double row of brass buttons on their black serge uniforms, hence the term "brassbounder." On board, between four and twelve "mercantile snotties" lived apart from the crew in separate accommodation called the half-deck. Under the law, they had officer status and were expected to take the captain's side in any dispute. In fact, they seldom had their hands out of the tar bucket. Apprentices worked all the hours God gave, pulling their weight — and more — alongside the seamen.

Perennially broke and half starved, apprentices made life hum with daredevil antics in far-flung ports. Some deserted because the life was too tough. In ports of California and Australia, others lit out for more promising opportunities or were shanghaied into other ships.

For all its faults, the system made a strong man out of many a weak boy. It made hardy, confident, dependable seamen. The half-decks of windjammers were filled with the future captains of great transatlantic liners. As sail went into decline, however, so did the steady supply of young officers of unimpeachable professional character. A master's ticket in sail was a sure passport to softer, better-paid jobs in steam. Many shipping companies and pilotage authorities insisted on sailing experience. But opportunities for young men to obtain any experience under canvas, let alone a master mariner's ticket, were quickly drying up.

Demand for sail-trained men in leading merchant fleets was so intense that a whole new future was opened for the sailing ship. The foundations were laid for a fleet of beautiful white-winged vessels built for the sole mission of providing the experience of seafaring under sail. Their cargo would be character. A new term entered the vocabulary of the sea — "sail training."

The concept developed in three overlapping phases. Initially, a number of shipowners turned to the training of cadet officers in ships that continued trading. The logical development of the apprentice system, it was the classical idea of sail training. Ships paid their way by carrying cargo but were manned by a large number of cadets paying to learn the job under the eyes of instructors.

One of the first companies to combine ocean trading with training was Devitt and Moore, a British company running passengers to Australia. In 1888 it converted two ships to carry one hundred cadets, each paying a premium of two hundred and fifty pounds for five voyages. After 1918 Great Britain, despite her maritime importance, never again trained seamen under sail. But other countries had a different view.

In 1901 the Norddeutscher-Lloyd company of Germany commissioned two large cargo carriers to train men for its own merchant fleet. The *Herzogin Cecilie* and the *Herzogin Sophie*, carrying sixty-six apprentices and fourteen hands, had no mechanical aids such as steam capstans or halyard winches.

Sweden had at least three Cape Horners manned largely by cadets. Navies, too, were recognizing the value of sail training. The Swedish Navy sent two hundred cadets on training voyages in the *A.F. Chapman*. The Argentine Navy commissioned the *Presidente Sarmiento* for the same purpose. From 1896, the Portuguese Navy used the former German *Rickmer Rickmers*, and in 1924 commissioned the first *Sagres*.

In 1907 Denmark built the four-masted barque *Viking* to train cadets while trading. She was sold in 1928 and replaced by the *Kobenhavn*, a five-masted barque with a small auxiliary engine.

Between the wars, a number of cadet ships traded under different flags. The *Archibald Russell*, one of the last windjammers in Great Britain, was bought by Gustav Erikson of Finland and refitted as a cadet ship to be used in the Australian grain trade. Finland also had the *Favell* and the *Fennia*, a French-built four-poster bought after she had been dismasted off the Horn and towed to the Falklands. Four of the last Laeisz vessels in Germany were fitted with berths for forty cadets apiece. Belgium had the four-masted barque *L'Avenir*. France also had a number of ships. One of them, the *Richelieu*, met a spectacular end in Baltimore when the pitch dust she was loading exploded. The era of classical sail training would not completely end until the *Pamir* went down in a hurricane in 1957, but the days of these beautiful, well-run ships were largely over by the mid-1930s.

Meanwhile, the second phase of sail training had been gaining momentum and it suddenly flourished. The idea of a sailing ship that carried no cargo but voyaged with the sole aim of building character and training seamen inspired one of the most unexpected phenomena of this technological age — the renaissance of sail.

Probably the first-ever "school ship" was the Swedish brig *Carl Johan*, commissioned in 1848. In 1881 Norway's small school-ship society was boosted with funds from a benefactor, which led to four successive training ships bearing his name, Christian Radich. In 1882 in Denmark, a philanthropist endowed funds for a small full-rigged ship to train young men for the merchant navy; she was named after his son, Georg Stage. Various navies were using small ships to train young officers, and their traditions of smartness were widely adopted.

At the turn of the century the German Schoolship Association was founded. In 1909 its first ship, the pretty *Grossherzogin Elisabeth*, started training voyages to the West Indies in summer and the Baltic in winter. Larger ships followed but were appropriated after the First World War and dispersed to different flags.

Then the whole tradition of sail training was revitalized with the vigorous rearmament programs of the Third Reich. Between 1933 and 1940 Germany built no less than five barques to train naval cadets. These vessels were dispersed to other countries after the Second World War. Though some are fragile with age, four are still sailing today. The *Gorch Fock*, built in 1933, dropped from sight in the Soviet Union to emerge in the 1950s as the *Tovarisch*. The *Horst Wessel* was taken over by the United States Coast Guard and renamed *Eagle*. The *Albert Leo Schlageter* was claimed by Brazil and was later transferred to Portuguese colors as the

Sailors work on the rigging aboard Port Jackson: *since doldrum calms cause heavy wear, the crew replaces best storm-weather canvas with old sails.*

Sagres II. The *Mircea* hoisted the Romanian flag. The fifth barque, *Herbert Norkus*, under construction when war broke out, was never rigged. West Germany reaffirmed her faith in sail training in 1958 by building a new barque, *Gorch Fock II*. Today these beautiful white-painted barques are known as the five sisters. At every opportunity they challenge each other to race for the Five Sisters Cup (currently held by *Gorch Fock II*). But *Tovarisch* and *Mircea* have been confined to the Black Sea for some years because their bones are aching; *Sagres II*, with the distinctive red crosses on her sails, is also feeling her age.

In the 1930s other countries were also building training vessels, which are still sailing. The ship *Danmark* was built in 1933 for the Danish merchant marine. A little smaller and carrying the youngest of all the crews, the full-rigger *Christian Radich* of Norway was launched in 1937. Denmark's *Georg Stage* was replaced by a new full-rigger in 1934 while the old ship, renamed *Joseph Conrad*, made an epic two-year voyage round the world in the hands of Alan Villiers. Italy's bulky *Amerigo Vespucci*, a rather different style of vessel with her gilded stern gallery and black-and-white hull stripes reminiscent of an old man-of-war, was built in 1931 to train naval cadets. Spain's massive *Juan Sebastian de Elcano*, launched in 1927 for naval training, was not a ship or barque like the others but a four-masted topsail schooner.

The revived interest in sail training after the Second World War prompted South American countries to build new vessels. First came

Chile's barquentine *Esmeralda* in 1952, and Argentina's ship *Libertad* in 1956. Then four similar barques came from the same yard in Spain: Colombia's *Gloria* in 1968, Ecuador's *Guayas* in 1978, Venezuela's *Simon Bolivar* in 1980, and the *Cuauhtemoc* for Mexico in 1982.

Meanwhile, two of the mightiest square-riggers that ever sailed returned to the scene as training ships under the Soviet flag. The *Kruzenshtern*, with her distinctive black-and-white checkered topsides, started life as the *Padua*, built as the last of the famous Flying P nitrate traders. The white *Sedov*, built in Germany in 1921 as the *Magdalene Vinnen*, virtually new after a five-year refit, is the biggest of today's fleet. Each carries about one hundred and sixty fisheries cadets.

Old salts who experienced the rigors of the real Cape Horn life might be excused for their scorn toward modern training ships. Compared with the old windjammer tramping the loneliest sea lanes with uninviting cargoes, the training ships are certainly different. Their holds are classrooms. Their silky scrubbed decks have never felt the wounding scrape of a hobnailed boot. They smell of Brasso and soap rather than sweat and toil. Ironwork shines with fresh paint. Every knot and splice seems to stand to attention, like their well-drilled crews who sing shanties rather than stamp and grunt them out in the old style. Crews are large and the workload per person is greatly reduced. The *Kruzenshtern*, handled by only thirty men and boys when she flogged around Cape Horn in the nitrate trade, is now sailed by two hundred and forty, and there are few calluses on the hands of the young Soviet cadets.

With no cargo to weigh them down, the square-riggers ride high in the water. It's unusual for green water to roar like an avalanche over the lee rail. Even when spooning along with a cap full of wind, there is always the hum of generators because electricity is required for radios, freezers, and air conditioning. Square-riggers today tend to be traditional from the deck up: their sailing gear relies entirely on muscle power. Below deck, however, they draw on everything technology can provide for fireproof materials, navigation instruments, and cooking equipment. *Eagle* even has a popcorn machine.

In classic sail training, cadets were taught to get used to bad weather, and they learned to master it. But no Tall Ship captain today courts bad weather if, by exercise of prudent seamanship and modern communication, he can avoid it. Most training ships lay up through harsh winter weather, or set a course for sunnier climes. It's rare that any square-rigger of today rounds one of the three southern capes — Cape Horn (Chile), the Cape of Good Hope (South Africa), or Cape Otway (Australia) — that were the familiar milestones of all ocean passage-making in the nineteenth century. With their many ventilators, companionways, and skylights, none of today's square-riggers could challenge the great seas and vast winds of the southern oceans.

Modern sail-training ships might sail with radar in the chart-house and a video screen in the messdeck, but the challenges their lofty spars offer to individuals are not one bit diminished. Instead of five perhaps it's fifty young men — and women — scrambling aloft to take in sail. But this does not lessen the whipcrack of the wind in their oilies, or steady the giddy sway of the spars to which they cling, or reduce their height. No matter how many hands in a watch, for every individual, cold sea water at five o'clock in the morning remains just as hellishly wet.

The sea does not change. It is the same now as in the days of the windjammers, as in clipper days, as in the days of the Vikings. The sea is the great leveler: the maker and breaker. At sea in a ship depending on nothing but wind, muscle, and teamwork, the individual confronts real life. And this is the spirit behind the third phase: sail training as a foundation for life.

This kind of sail training has little to do with teaching sailing but everything to do with using the sea-going experience to develop character. It is a training *by* the sea rather than *for* the sea. Starting in European countries, later in North America, New Zealand, Australia, and other countries, organizations were established to provide young people with opportunities to undergo a concentrated experience of seafaring under sail. The primary purpose was to help them taste something of that jubilation of the Horn — that struggle with something bigger than themselves — thereby building self-esteem and confidence.

A new breed of Tall Ship sailed on short voyages in pursuit of the same spirit of adventure and exultation as their larger square-rigged sisters. In Canada, Francis A. MacLachlan designed, built, and then commanded the first of three 60-foot brigantines: *St. Lawrence II* in 1952, *Pathfinder* in 1962, and *Playfair* in 1973. These ships still train young crews of the Great Lakes. Great Britain launched the 134-foot, three-masted topsail schooner *Sir Winston Churchill* in 1966; her sister ship, *Malcolm Miller*, came two years later. In 1971 the 76-foot brig *Royalist*, known by the Russians as "mini-Kruzenshtern" because of her black-and-white topsides, was built for Britain's sea cadets. The 107-foot schooner *Eendracht* of the Netherlands followed in 1974, then the Irish brigantine *Asgard II* in 1979.

The same principles of exposing individuals to testing situations were also found to be effective on shorter voyages in yachts. The sail-training "family" began to embrace a great number of other small vessels, which explains why many of the vessels in Tall Ships Races are not especially tall. Today, the term *Tall Ship* includes all vessels from the great *Sedov* of the Soviet Union to the little *Olifant* of West Germany, sailed by two elderly men and three boys. But they ply the same trade. Their cargo is character.

The idea of bringing together all ships embodying the traditions, craftsmanship, and daring of sail was initiated in 1956 by Bernard Morgan, not a professional sailor but a solicitor in England who loved sailing ships. That summer, twenty-one sail-training vessels from eleven countries set off from Torbay, in Devon, England, and sailed to Lisbon, Portugal, in the "last" great race of sailing ships.

Unlike the tea-clipper races and others that developed on the spur of the moment when rivals sighted each other on the open ocean, this was a properly organized event. The race was started and finished with the bang of a gun. A guard-ship accompanied the fleet in case of accidents. Cheerful festivals of flags, sports, shanties, and parties were laid on for the ships' young crews in harbor.

The event caught the imagination of sailors and lovers of ships. Far from being the last race, it was really the first. Morgan's committee formed itself into the Sail Training Association (STA), and a race committee of Tall Ship captains decided races would be organized for the big square-riggers every second year.

In 1964, the Tall Ships fleet raced across the Atlantic for the first time, from Lisbon to Bermuda. The event was so popular that races began to be held annually. Races for square-riggers were still staged in even-numbered years while the rapidly growing fleet of smaller vessels raced every year.

In 1976 came an event that put Tall Ships Races into world focus. The European fleet raced from England to Bermuda, where the vessels met with other ships sailing up from South America. The combined fleet of sixteen square-riggers raced to Newport, Rhode Island, then cruised in company to New York. The parade of sail there, watched by millions from the skyscraper windows of Manhattan and by many more millions on television, was the high point of America's bicentennial celebrations. Ten years later the fleet — increased to twenty-six square-riggers — again paraded in New York, to salute the Statue of Liberty.

A key element in race programs are the crew exchanges when trainees from most vessels exchange berths. As in the old days when numerous nationalities would be found in a windjammer's fo'c'sle, language and custom make little difference at sea. The shared experience of a good shake-up over salt water brings people together. There can be no shyness between those who have been soused by the same wave, vomited over the side together, and hauled on the same rope.

The ships are welcomed wherever they go. Cities queue up to receive them because of the economic benefits they bring. Visitors are counted in the millions. When six square-riggers and a hundred smaller vessels gathered in Boston, two million people poured into the city every day to see them. Crews were marooned on board by the press of people. A state of emergency was declared and the National Guard turned out to control crowds and traffic.

These white-winged vessels are more than mere ships; they are national symbols. The Norwegian ship *Christian Radich* crossed the Atlantic in 1986 at the invitation of a president. The role of ambassador is one that sailing ships wear well and with pride. Says Captain Ernst Cummings of the U.S. Coast Guard barque *Eagle*: "If a nation wants to send a friendly signal, how much better for it to be carried by a graceful wind ship crewed by young people than by some nuclear-powered carrier or battleship."

6 The Smile at the End of the Storm

Why do men voyage under sail but for these great moments of self-confidence?
JOSEPH CONRAD

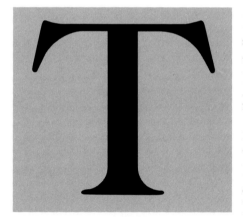

THERE'S NOTHING like the sight of a line of Tall Ships to take the heart back a few decades. From every sternjack and lofty yardarm, colored flags rattle in the breeze. Decks dry to a pale silkiness after their morning scrub; varnished brightwork gleams. Ropes hang in careful coils on every belaying pin. Aloft, the sails have had a tight harbor stow and every yard is exactly squared. The gilded gingerbread scrollwork decorating escutcheons and nameboards reflects prettily on the water. From every quarterdeck, on the hour and half hour, the gleaming brass bell rings out the ageless time-chimes of the sea.

In every vessel the suntanned and windblown young men and women have a strikingly confident way about them. Some wear sailors' uniforms; others wear knitted pullovers or T-shirts with their ship's name across the chest. All wear a special look of pride, which is at least as memorable and touching, in its way, as the romantic spectacle of square-rigged ships. They have seen a different world.

At the spectacular festivals of sail generated by gatherings of the family of Tall Ships, the spirit of youth, enterprise, and beauty flies masthead-high. Few of the thousands — often millions — of sightseers fail to be moved by it.

Hours later, after the ships are gone, a gust of wind rattles the window but you turn over in a comfortable bed and drift back to sleep. On board the Tall Ships, however, the romance of the sea takes a different twist.

At sea, as old sailors would say, it's blowing scissors and thumbscrews. Thorns of cold spray fly in the wind. Every few seconds a black void opens beneath the ship's bows and she falls into it. You learn what it feels like to ride a roller coaster while balancing on a stepladder. First the sickening plunge into a wall of water which buckles the knees, then the soaring swoop over the back of the wave, which lifts your clammy boots off the deck. Just as you realize your stomach and brain have changed places, there is a drenching bomb-burst of icy water.

It's not a scene commonly found on posters of beautiful ships sailing on sparkling seas. What calendar picture captures the chill numbness of raw fingers, the sticky prickle of damp clothing, the death wish engendered by a desperately heaving stomach, the thunderous din of a sailing ship roiling through toppling seas? Voyaging under sail has little to do with shanties and hot cocoa, and everything to do with sweat, cold, fear, sickness, and bloody blisters — and with the intensely personal business of being put through the wringer and emerging pale, damp, and triumphant, a tried and proven individual.

The moment you step on board as a new crew member of a square-rigger, schooner, or sloop, the world seems to shrink. Nothing exists beyond the stanchions or bulwarks bounding the deck. The masts and spars, which seem to fill the sky, are a puzzle: shrouds, halyards, downhauls, topping lifts, outhauls, reef-points, buntlines, clewlines, mainsheet, braces.... The rig is a nautical poem to be crammed into your brain. Until every rope is learned and you can find them all unhesitatingly by touch, the ship may not sail. But the learning comes easily when you are putting your weight on the tail of a rope and seeing for yourself how they all fit together.

Below, you're assigned a narrow bunk or shown how to sling a hammock from hooks in the deck beams. Clothing and other gear are stowed in a small locker. The crew is split into two teams called watches, usually two or three. While one works on deck the others clean, cook, and sleep. Watch-leaders drill new hands in safety, sail-handling, and how to work the lifeboat should somebody fall over the side. But there's more to seafaring than nautical crafts. You also do your share of scrubbing, cleaning pots and pans, and taking turns at what Cape Horners called "doing peg," fetching food for your shipmates.

A Tall Ship is not a museum but a working vessel. Pulling on a rope is not good enough: you must exert every muscle, and not in your own sweet time but in unison with others. Pulling on a rope may not seem a meaningful experience but its effect is obvious: the sail catches the wind and you can feel the thrust of it as the deck heels under your feet. It's your own work making the ship go.

Going aloft for the first time, some are fearless and some tremble every inch of the way. The more "up-and-overs" you do the easier it gets. Forearms ache with the effort of clinging with unnecessary exertion. Old hands call it the death grip. Scrambling aloft to let a topsail out of its ties,

True grit, Cape Horn style: men hauling on a rope are washed off their feet by an avalanche of water as they fight their ship around the Cape of Storms.

you find the mast is swaying giddily. But it's not good enough just to inch out on the footrope and hang on like grim death: there's a job to be done. The canvas is snapped into billows by the wind. It is an untamed and powerful thing, like a wild horse.

Nothing is more enchanting in all seafaring than the moment when the engine is shut down and the old girl begins to sail. All is smooth, sweet, and thrilling. The deck tilts as the wind punches the canvas into galleon curves. Your fingers are pinched into the sore beginnings of Cape Horn calluses. Spray flies over the bow as the ship drives her shoulder into the small inshore seas. The wake points a foam-flecked finger at the land from which you've come. Home grows smaller by the minute.

Navigators take compass bearings of lighthouses and landmarks. Their penciled crosses on the chart show the ship's track striding out into open water. As the broad horizon beckons you begin to feel every inch an old salt, welcoming the spirited lift of the bow over the first broad-backed ocean swell. The captain decides to tack, altering course to bring the wind on the other side of the vessel.

There is a flurry of hectic activity. All hell seems to break loose. The sails thunder and rattle. Sheets and blocks flail as if intent on crushing your skull. You pull on this and heave on that. The helm is put over and the ship comes into the eye of the wind, lunging heavily into head seas. Every tilt and angle reverses itself. The sails crack full of wind and the ship heels over in the opposite direction then tramps away on the other tack. Sheets and braces are heaved taut all over again, with more toil and sweat. You're outward bound in a deep-waterman, setting a course for foreign parts.

At dusk, the ship is bowling along under plain sail. With something of a thudding heart, you realize she is sailing out of the calendar picture into the real thing. The wind is building up and you can hear the boom of it in the rigging. There are a few tons of weight in the sails now. The high yards are swinging like trapeze bars under the big top of the angry sky. Word spreads from the chart-house: a gale is coming.

The navigation lights are switched on. As the night deepens, flying spray glows eerily red and green as it is caught in their glow. Supper is a trial. Below, it's bedlam. Every locker not properly latched has flung its entire contents across the deck. The bilge water slopping beneath the floor wafts a thick, oily odor into the stuffy air. Ventilators are closed because of the threatening storm. Shadows sway strangely as lamps tilt in their gimbals with the pitch and sway of the ship.

Seasickness can be a nightmare for the afflicted. Of every five people one is never touched by it, one always is, and the other three are affected to varying degrees. Seasickness comes in two stages. First you think you're dying, then you want to die. It's a miserable business but brings no dishonor. What matters is how you cope with it. In a sailing ship it's impossible to cave in. Too many people depend on you. Your own survival depends on other people and you have to trust them. At the same time you have to be dependable because others trust in you. Hence the reasoning. A voyage under sail is a training for life. Sail training is a cheap way of making dependable people.

"When I say pull—pull yer hearts out!"
Heavy work for cadets and crew in Port
Jackson, *about 1913.*

Sail training comes in as many guises as there are different rigs and
vessels. The large square-riggers, most of them owned by national navies,
merchant-marine academies, or coast guards, are run on military lines.
Cadets are taught basic professional skills while getting a raw taste of the
elements in which they will spend their careers. Driving a modern ship,
whether it carries missiles or containers, is an indoor collar-and-tie job
with hardly a taste of salt spray passing the lips. Without a concentrated
experience in a sailing ship, young officers in responsible posts might
never know at first hand what they were taking on. Lessons learned at sea
under sail are never forgotten. In these ships the emphasis is on discipline, teamwork, and formal instruction. It's primarily a training *for*
the sea.

Other schemes, however, throw the emphasis on education *by* the sea. In
smaller sail-training vessels, like the British, Dutch, and Irish schooners,
voyages lasting about two weeks are geared to provide young crew
members with the opportunity to discover self-reliance through adventure
on the sea. What they do not provide is a training in sail, with classes in

astronomical navigation and tests on practical work with a marlinespike, though enthusiastic interest in matters of seamanship is always rewarding. It's easy to say that in these ships nautical skills come second to a high-sounding affair called character building, but a lot harder to define exactly what that priority is.

Just as apprentice Cape Horners did, and generations of ships' boys before them, the young people on the Tall Ships discover a capacity for endurance, perseverance, and cheerfulness against the odds. A sailing ship deliberately imposes testing situations on individuals. Its challenges are not simulated but real. You might be scared to death, but overcoming your fears does wonders for your self-respect.

The process gets tough around midnight on the first night at sea. The novelty wore off hours ago. You are feeling sick, exhausted, and frightened. You feel as though you have been bucketing around the ocean all your life. Land must be a million miles away, if it exists at all. And the weather is worsening.

In the violent motion, it's a sweat even to stand still and vertical without a minor feat of acrobatics. Muscles complain, as though you had been jogging all day. For hours you ache for the release from the bitter wind and driving spray that midnight will bring, when you can crawl into a cozy sleeping bag and close your eyes. When at last the other watch staggers blearily on deck to relieve you, your bunk is on the uphill, windward side and sloping toward you at shoulder level at an angle of twenty degrees. With spinning head, you rig the weather-cloth to hold you in. Water slurps along the hull just a few inches from your ear. It gurgles in the bilges, boils up over the rail, seethes in the scuppers, floods across the deck, splatters into the taut canvas of the sails. The spray rattles into the sails and hisses on the waves; the sails make a fluted hum. The deck is a drum magnifying every footstep, every slap and creak.

Down below, clothes hanging from pegs scrape back and forth. Pencils roll. Fuel and fresh water gulp in the tanks. Tins and jars knock and rattle in the galley lockers. Boots, books, and even bananas scull about. You doze in snatches, perhaps between intervals of gruesome retching, and your four hours of "watch below" are soon gone.

Water is never wetter than when it slashes into your face as you come blinking on deck at four in the morning. It runs down your neck with all the mercy of liquid hailstones. It's too late now for the towel you should have knotted tightly around your throat. The only light is a faint glow from the compass. Then your eyes begin to adjust and the darkness is filled with the pale shadows of wave-crests peaking above the level of the rail, the sails stretched to the wind, the faces of other crew members as they feel their way around you.

It's your turn for lookout duty in the bow. Praying for the comfort of dawn, you cling to the forestay and stare into the blackness, blinking sleep away and dreading that you'll fail to see the vast bulk of some supertanker bearing down on a collision course. The wind hammers your clothing flat. Then a tap on the shoulder, an encouraging grin from beneath a bright orange hood shining wetly, and a mug of something hot is thrust in your hands. Cocoa or soup? Hard to tell, but who cares?

At last a gray horizon grows out of the darkness. One moment it's cut in two by the bowsprit spearing up into the heavens, then it joins again as the bow plummets into the trough, leaving you momentarily weightless in space. As your body catches up and begins to drop, it meets the deck on its way up. The daylight reveals an unbroken vista of spilling crests: an empty wilderness of black-and-white hills.

Four bells is sounded: six o'clock. Duties rotate, and you take the wheel. Steering a sailing ship through heavy seas when her hat is full of wind is a sport fit for gods. It can be hard work, and it takes time to get the knack. The whole vessel seems like a living thing. You feel as if you are holding the ship's heart in your hands. With red and hollow eyes, you watch the seas unfold on the bow, watch the flutter of the leech near the head of the jib, watch the telltale, a black ribbon tied in the shrouds to indicate wind direction, watch the compass, watch the burgee fluttering at the masthead where it catches the first rays of sun.

Your own palms on the spokes of her wheel, the ship soars over the heaving waves, graceful as a gull. The waves peak so high alongside you can look right into their jade-green depths. Through your trick on the wheel, your stomach doesn't heave once. At seven bells, the other watch comes up. There's a whiff of coffee on the air as the promised gale is poised to break over the ship. With all hands on deck at the change of watch, the captain prudently decides to reduce sail. The watch-leader marshals his men. "Main topsail it is, lads and lasses. Aloft and stow!"

With hardly a thought for the romantic posters of sailing ships that landed you in this gut-churning predicament, you climb up the ratlines. Over the futtock shrouds and up the topmast you go, nerves somehow held together by the impetus of action. The next person's boots are in front of your eyes; you sense the knuckles of the person coming up behind. No opportunity for hesitation, no time to think and worry.

Moving gingerly from shrouds to yard, you notice one shipmate who seems even more scared. You help him or her find handholds, and your own confidence soars. The sail billows and flaps around your ears. In the sweat of getting the job done, you grab the sail in a bear hug, thrust it under your belly, then lie on it. Over the top of the yard you get a dizzy view of water, far below.

It's a long, grueling day, harder than anything you have ever known. During the forenoon watch comes your stint of cleaning below decks. Lunch is a joke. The dry biscuits sloshed down with tea slosh up again ten minutes later. The seas are big and ugly. Lifelines are rigged across the deck. During the first dogwatch it rains, but you haven't forgotten the towel around your neck this time. By dark you're so exhausted it's all you can do to stay on your feet.

The captain, experienced and wise, knows that seasickness and exhaustion are an important part of the training. This is life at sea, the wild motion, the seasickness, the work. You can't sit down just because you feel tired: you must find the inner reserves and measure up. Discipline doesn't have to be taught or imposed: the need for it is self-evident. In a basic world of wind, sea, and survival, you learn what life is all about in ways you will never forget.

The value of such experience is impossible to quantify in terms of conventional education. What schoolroom could substitute for this fight with the sea? But in sail training there is no balance sheet of passes and failures. Young people come aboard the ships tense, awkward, apprehensive, knowing nothing about the ship and less about the sea. They hardly know what has hit them. The captain sees them growing up. The experience molds them into a crew, a team whose bond is the ship.

The magic begins to exert itself in the midnight-to-four-o'clock watch during the second storm-tossed night. Standing a lonely lookout duty, you suddenly find you are singing.

The bite has gone out of the wind. The rise and fall of the deck is hardly noticed; your muscles ride it automatically. A wafer of moon breaking through the clouds lays a wriggling silver track on the waves. A few luckless shipmates still hang their heads over the rail, but now they are running sweepstakes on who will be next to throw up. From another group sheltering in the lee of the galley, breathing in the smells of hot bread wafting from its scuttles, comes the sound of a mouth organ playing "Blow the Man Down." Life begins again.

After your watch, you sleep like a rock. Morning brings dry clothes and a good breakfast. When you go on deck, you find the ship is snoring along under a sky blue enough to patch the dungarees of a whole navy. The other watch has set more sail and scrubbed down, but there's more work to be done. The climb up into the rigging holds no terrors for you now. With seasickness gone and the black waves of the long nights quickly forgotten, your shipmates are in high spirits. You are pleased to be one of them, proud to have been tested by the sea and not found wanting, happy to be a sailor in a Tall Ship.

The smile at the end of the storm says everything about sail training.

LEFT: *Crew climb aloft on the mainmast of* Illawarra, *built 1881, a British ship on the Australia run that carried a large crew of cadets who paid a premium for a training under sail.*

RIGHT: *Heavy work in* Gorch Fock II *as cadets struggle with the headsails.*

RACING THE TALL SHIPS

LEFT: Dar Mlodziezy *logs an amazing seventeen and a half knots during part of the race from Bermuda to Halifax; lifelines are rigged on her maindeck for protection from seas breaking aboard.*

ABOVE: *"Mainsail haul!" Watching for the lift of the sails, an* Eagle *cadet gives the critical order that will put the ship on the other tack.*

FOLLOWING PAGES: *Jostling for starting positions in the race from Newcastle upon Tyne to Bremerhaven: the Irish brigantine* Asgard II *and the giant Polish ship* Dar Mlodziezy.

LEFT: *One of the last of the bona fide Cape Horners, the four-masted barque Kruzenshtern, which trains Soviet fishery cadets, was built in 1926 to ply the South American nitrate trade. She is seen here off Newcastle upon Tyne, England.*

Nothing is done the push-button way in training vessels like the Gorch Fock II *except in matters of safety such as fire protection and navigation. The rest is sweat, tears, and blisters. There's no room for slackers or the faint-hearted when there's work to be done (right). Those who don't look lively get stamped on. Even the officers who shout the orders (below) have worked their way up the hard way.*

The gaff schooner Hoshi *(right), of Britain's Island Cruising Club, has a bone in her teeth at the start of the Cutty Sark Tall Ships Race from Chatham to Zeebrugge. In the same race was one of the smallest in the Tall Ships fleet and a regular race contestant: the* Olifant *(above) of West Germany. Sailed by only two men and three trainees, the thirty-eight-foot cutter, built in 1977, is a replica of a Danish coastal trader.*

FOLLOWING PAGES: *"Two, six, heave!" is the cry aboard the topsail schooner* Malcolm Miller *as a mixed crew claps on sail.*

ABOVE: Lookouts double up as Dar Mlodziezy *is shrouded in fog while racing from Bermuda to Halifax, Nova Scotia; watch is also kept by radar.*

RIGHT: Royalist *snores along with a cap full of wind, her young crew sweating to squeeze the last fraction of a knot out of their beautiful little brig.*

FOLLOWING PAGES: The school ship Grossherzogin Elisabeth, *of West Germany, is a three-masted schooner with accommodation for about sixty merchant navy cadets in deckhouses on an elegant hull.*

Red Maltese crosses mark the square sails of the Portuguese barque Sagres II *(left). Cadets (above) man the wheel.*

The view from the main top (below): Libertad *of Argentina snores along through sunlit seas. For her transatlantic run made in six days, twenty-one hours, the ship won the Boston Teapot Trophy (left), mounted outside the wardroom.*

Navigation: The Rough-and-Ready Art

It was far more difficult to navigate a sailing ship in the nineteenth century than it is to find your way at sea in a small yacht today. The safety and performance of a ship depended more on the captain's ability and skill and on his nose for trouble than on anything else. Even if a shipmaster did have more than a sketchy notion of how to find his position at sea by the sun, moon, and stars, accuracy was impossible.

A captain was expected to provide his own navigation equipment and charts. It was common even for a crack clipper to voyage around the globe by way of Australia with only half a dozen charts of such a small scale that the width of a pencil mark could represent a hundred miles or more. In any case, before the age of satellite imagery even the most scientific of position-fixing was rudimentary and the land itself was often charted up to ten miles out of position on the Earth's surface.

To find his latitude the typical shipmaster would "shoot" the angle of the sun at noon by sextant, but this depended on being able to see the sun. If he was lucky his sight would be accurate to within a couple of miles. Few bothered with star sights and other, more complicated figuring.

Finding longitude depended on knowing the exact time at Greenwich. The captain carried an expensive chronometer in a baize-lined box, and made a ceremony of carefully winding it up every day, but it was only a clockwork mechanism vulnerable to heat, cold, humidity, and the motion of the sea. Every morning at Deal, in Kent, where outward-bound ships anchored to await fair winds, a black ball was lowered from a tower at precisely eight o'clock so ships' clocks could be adjusted. But once they had sailed it might be years before a reliable time-check could be made: there were no radio signals.

With all these uncertainties it was hardly surprising that master and mate kept their navigation plots under lock and key while at sea and never let out the ship's position, even to the other mates. Typically, the men before the mast seldom knew their ship's position to within a thousand miles. But they would know from the captain's anxiety and perhaps the twitching of his nose when landfall was nigh.

In a modern training ship like the U.S. Coast Guard's *Eagle*, trainee navigation teams work around the clock. The barque might be sail-powered but in seconds her position can be pinpointed to within a few meters. One system linked to satellites gives an instant read-out of latitude and longitude. Another is linked to special radio transmitters a-shore. Radar gives a continuous picture of other ships and the nearby coastline. Cadets also navigate the hard way, with sextant sights and shorebearings.

But imagine what it must have been like for a captain making a landfall in not-so-distant days. Be it Cape Cod in Massachusetts, The Lizard in England, or Cape Horn itself, the problems were the same. His last reliable sun-sight might be ten days old. Ever since, his ship has been scudding before a gale under overcast skies. The chronometer is erratic; who can tell the extent of its error after a voyage halfway around the globe? The ship might be within ten miles of the captain's guess, or it might be two hundred miles farther on, liable in the next instant to pile up on some granite shore.

From his last reliable "fix" the captain plots his progress by "dead reckoning." On the chart he draws in the direction that the ship has steered, obtained from the compass, and from the ship's speed he works out how many miles have been covered.

To measure the speed the master orders, "Heave the log!" The log is a conical canvas bag or frame attached to a long thin line on a reel. The line is knotted at certain intervals. The log is dropped over the stern into the ship's wake and the first few fathoms of line are allowed to reel out so it settles. When the mate reaches a certain rag spliced into the line he calls out, "Turn!"

A seaman then turns a sandglass that measures a precise number of seconds, usually fourteen or twenty-eight. During this time the mate counts the number of knots running out through his fingers, each knot representing one nautical mile per hour. To this day a ship's speed is reckoned in knots. A note of the ship's direction and speed at different times through the day was kept on a slate in the main cabin, checked by the captain, and every twenty-four

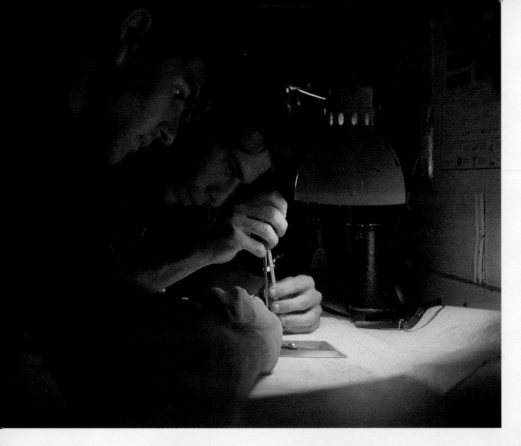

Tall ships are traditional from the deck up but every modern device is employed to ensure safety: in Eagle's navigation center, cadets use radar to ensure she is not on a collision course with any nearby ships. They also plot the ship's present position in the more traditional way, by laboring over the navigation chart in both Eagle (right) and Libertad (left).

School ships like Eagle place high value on the traditional skills of the mariner; cadets learning to navigate the hard way shoot the sun's angle by sextant.

hours recorded formally in the ship's logbook by the mate.

But dead reckoning was only as good as the helmsmen's ability to steer the desired course. It also had to make allowance for leeway, the sideways slip of a ship at sea, and for currents. But some of these factors were unknown. Over a period of days, huge errors could accumulate. Was the ship in fact where the captain had penciled a cross on the chart, or miles away?

When calculations, sixth sense, and the color of the water told the captain he was closing with the land he ordered a cast of the lead. The lead-line was a seven-pound lead weight hurled ahead of the ship. As it plummeted to the bottom a thin line, marked at certain depth intervals by scraps of leather and fabric, was dragged over the side. As the line came upright the depth was measured. When the lead was "armed" with tallow it brought up a sample of the

sand, shingle, or mud from the seabed. But the log was no help to a ship sailing fast and could not be used in deep water. Few captains worth their salt wasted a good breeze by taking in sail and heaving-to merely to assuage their own uncertainty.

It took nerve to keep driving on, plunging through fog or darkness and sometimes both, when at any moment the lookout might cry, "Breakers ahead!" By then it was usually too late. Even a clipper ship, let alone an unwieldy windjammer, required a lot of sea room in which to maneuver. In thick weather, if rocks or shoals were visible ahead, they spelled doom.

But more often the cry would be "Land ho!" The captain, after chewing his mustache with uncertainty over the past days, hell for the mates to live with, would scrutinize the distant shore then sagely nod his head. "Humph...just where I expected."

FOLLOWING PAGES: As the sun goes down, cadets practice taking star shots by sextant from Eagle's *foredeck.*

A Training in Sail

LEFT: *Taking a compass bearing of a landmark to obtain a navigational fix: an officer of the watch in* Sagres II.

ABOVE: *Every cadet stands a "trick" on the wheel and it can be hard work, especially in heavy weather;* Eagle's *bos'n keeps an eye on how the job's being done.*

FOLLOWING PAGES: *Lookout duty forward in* Gorch Fock II: *the presence of any vessel, land, or navigation mark is reported to the officer of the watch.*

Orders for the day are issued (right) by the executive officer as Gorch Fock II *sails across a smooth North Sea. When there's deckwork to be done (above), each cadet must pull more than his own weight and do more than his fair share, or the job won't get done.*

Learning the Ropes

H ALYARDS HOIST THE sails, downhauls bring them down again. Buntlines, leechlines, and clewlines gather the square sails up to their spars. Tacks and sheets control the bottom corners of the sail. Braces swing the whole yard around on the mast. Then there are preventers, vangs, inhauls, and outhauls, not to mention gantlines, clew garnets, lifts, and timenoguys...

A three-masted barque like *Eagle* has five miles of wire and rope in her rigging. More than 170 different lines control the set of the sails. If you don't know the main upper topsail inner buntline from the mizzen topgallant staysail downhaul you can hardly call yourself a sailor.

The rig is a nautical poem to be crammed into the brain. Cadets must quickly learn to find every rope instantly and by touch, even on the darkest, wettest night. Ships' officers are strict about it. To throw off a wrong rope could damage the ship or, even worse, injure a shipmate aloft.

Every rope comes down to a belaying pin slotted into the rail on either side of the deck, or the fife rail at the foot of each mast. The system is not as complicated as it looks. The square-rigged masts are virtually identical. In general, the higher the sail, the farther aft its lines will be.

Getting down to the job, a cadet in Eagle *prepares for the all-important pinrail test; 100 percent accuracy is demanded.*

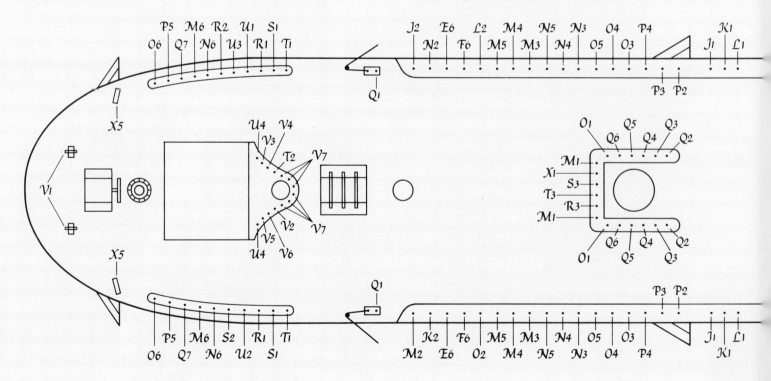

A. Flying Jib
1. Sheet
2. Halyard
3. Downhaul

B. Outer Jib
1. Sheet
2. Halyard
3. Downhaul

C. Inner Jib
1. Sheet
2. Halyard
3. Downhaul

D. Fore Topmast Staysail
1. Sheet
2. Halyard
3. Downhaul

E. Fore Royal
1. Sheet
2. Halyard
3. Clewline
4. Buntline
5. Leechline
6. Brace

F. Fore Topgallant
1. Sheet
2. Halyard
3. Clewline
4. Buntline
5. Leechline
6. Brace

G. Fore Upper Topsail
1. Sheet
2. Halyard
3. Clewline
4. Inner Buntline
5. Outer Buntline
6. Brace

H. Fore Lower Topsail
1. Sheet
2. Cleatline
3. Inner Buntlines
4. Outer Buntlines
5. Brace

I. Foresail
1. Fore Sheet Bitt
2. Forelift
3. Fore Leechline
4. Fore Inner Buntline
5. Fore Outer Buntline
6. Brace

J. Main Royal Staysail
1. Sheet
2. Halyard
3. Downhaul

K. Main Topgallant Staysail
1. Sheet
2. Halyard
3. Downhaul

L. Main Topmast Staysail
1. Sheet
2. Halyard
3. Downhaul

M. Main Royal
1. Sheet
2. Halyard
3. Clewline
4. Buntline
5. Buntleechline
6. Brace

N. Main Topgallant
1. Sheet
2. Halyard
3. Clewline
4. Buntline
5. Buntleechline
6. Brace

O. Main Upper Topsail
1. Sheet
2. Halyard
3. Clewline
4. Inner Buntline
5. Outer Buntline
6. Brace

P. Main Lower Topsail
1. Sheet
2. Clewline
3. Inner Buntline
4. Outer Buntline
5. Brace

Q. Mainsail
1. Sheet Bitts
2. Clew Garnet
3. Lift
4. Leechline
5. Inner Buntline
6. Outer Buntline
7. Brace

R. Mizzen Topgallant Staysail
1. Sheet
2. Halyard
3. Downhaul

S. Mizzen Topmast Staysail
1. Sheet
2. Halyard
3. Downhaul

T. Mizzen Staysail
1. Sheet
2. Halyard
3. Downhaul

U. Gaff Topsail
1. Sheet
2. Halyard
3. Clew
4. Tack

V. Spanker
1. Sheets
2. Topping Lift
3. Foot Outhaul
4. Foot Inhaul
5. Peak Outhaul
6. Peak Inhaul
7. Brails

X. Other
1. Gantlines
2. Clew Garnets
3. Lazy Tack Bits
4. Main Tack Jigger
5. Vang

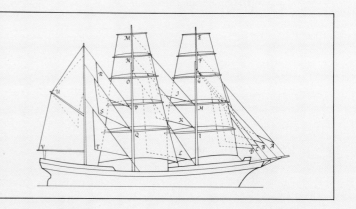

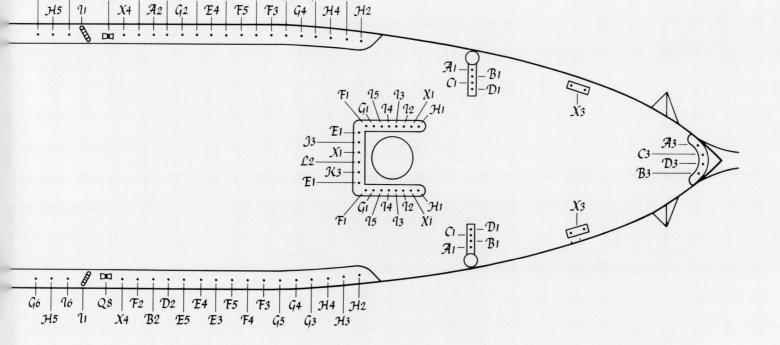

FACING THE CHALLENGE

THE BRIG *Royalist* is one of the smallest of the square-riggers in the Tall Ships fleet and carries one of the youngest crews. The first square-rigger built to fly the British flag in more than half a century, she was launched in 1971 for the Sea Cadet Corps. Voyaging in nearly all weathers from February to November, she sails mostly with mixed crews of about twenty-two cadets on six-day trips in the English Channel and Southwest Approaches. But she also participates in Tall Ships Races and was outright winner of the race from Falmouth, England, to Lisbon, Portugal, in 1982. Once every three years or so she makes a circumnavigation of Great Britain.

The purpose of the ship is to take the maximum number of Sea Cadets offshore every year for tough, disciplined training in moderately rigorous conditions. To enable her to fulfill this role, the brig was deliberately fitted with square sails for the simple reason that this rig provides more jobs for more people than any other. The ship cannot be sailed without many pairs of willing hands to throw their weight on sheets, braces, halyards, buntlines, clewlines, and so on. Yet none of the sails is so big that a handful of young people cannot handle it when directed by an experienced officer.

The necessity of going aloft or of working out on a bowsprit spearing into the waves provides young people with challenging environments in which to discover their own unsuspected reserves of determination and fortitude. About seven hundred young people aged between thirteen and eighteen sail in *Royalist* every year, and no matter how miserable the trip, virtually every one of them wants to sign on for another trip the following year.

The ship is run on navy-style discipline. Cadets are divided into four watches. At sea, the deck is run by only five or six cadets, so they have lots to do with lookout duties, steering, and other jobs. More hands are called when sails have to be handled. Elementary instruction in sailing and seamanship is given while under way. Every cadet works for a qualification. First-trippers try to qualify for an offshore badge; offshore badgemen work to be rated offshore seaman; in turn, those who already have this qualification work to become watch leader. Many cadets who work their way up through the system return as adult watch officers.

Though her rig is traditional, *Royalist* makes much use of modern technology. The 4,660 square feet of working sail — all man-made sailcloth — is set on alloy masts and spars. The hull is steel, though the deck is laid teak. Radar and radio-navigation devices help the captain to keep the ship safe in crowded sea lanes on a dangerous coast. There are two auxiliary diesel engines. In ideal conditions, with the wind near the beam, the brig sails faster than twelve knots (fourteen miles per hour).

LEFT: *Preparing to throw off a line from the pinrail in* Dar Mlodziezy, *a cadet snatches a thoughtful look aloft to check he has found the correct one.*

RIGHT: *With deck watches, ship's work, and classes, the routine leaves little free time. Cadets are divided into four watches. One watch is always on deck, day and night, whether under sail or in port.*

TIME	AT SEA	ROUTINE	IN HARBOUR
0 6 6 0		CALL THE COOK	
0 5 5 0		O.O.W. RECORDS WEATHER FORECAST	
0 6 1 5	0 6 0 0	CALL THE COXN	
0 6 3 0		CALL THE HANDS	
0 6 5 0		HANDS MUSTER	
0 7 0 0			MESSMEN + FORENOON BREAKFAST
0 7 1 0	MESSMEN TO MESSDECK		
0 7 2 0	MESSMEN + FORENOON BREAKFAST		
0 7 3 0			HANDS TO BREAKFAST
0 7 5 0	FORENOON WATCH MUSTER		COLOUR PARTY MUSTER
0 8 0 0	HANDS TO BREAKFAST		COLOURS – CLEANING STATIONS
0 8 2 5		O.O.W. CALLS CAPTAIN FOR RADIO WATCH	
0 8 3 0		HANDS TO WORK OR INSTRUCTION	
0 9 4 5		STAND EASY	
1 0 0 0		HANDS TURN TO	
1 0 1 0		O.O.W. CALLS CAPTAIN FOR RADIO WATCH	
1 1 0 0		MESSMEN TO THE MESSDECK	
1 1 2 0		MESSMEN + AFTERNOON WATCH TO DINNER	
1 1 5 0		AFTERNOON WATCH MUSTER	
1 2 0 0		HANDS TO DINNER	
1 2 4 0		MAKE + MEND	
1 3 5 0		O.O.W. RECORDS WEATHER FORECAST	
1 5 0 0		HANDS TO TEA	
1 5 5 0		FIRST DOGWATCH TO MUSTER	
1 6 0 0		HANDS TO INSTRUCTION	
1 7 1 0		MESSMEN TO THE MESSDECK	
1 7 2 0		MESSMEN + LAST DOGWATCH TO SUPPER	
1 7 4 5		LAST DOGWATCH TO MUSTER. O.O.W. RECORDS WEATHER FCST	
1 8 0 0		HANDS TO SUPPER	
1 9 5 0		FIRST WATCH TO MUSTER	
2 0 0 0		HANDS PIPE DOWN (QUIET BELOW DECKS)	
2 1 5 0		MESSDECK ROUNDS	
2 2 0 0		HANDS TURN IN	
2 2 1 5		LIGHTS OUT	

DAY ONE

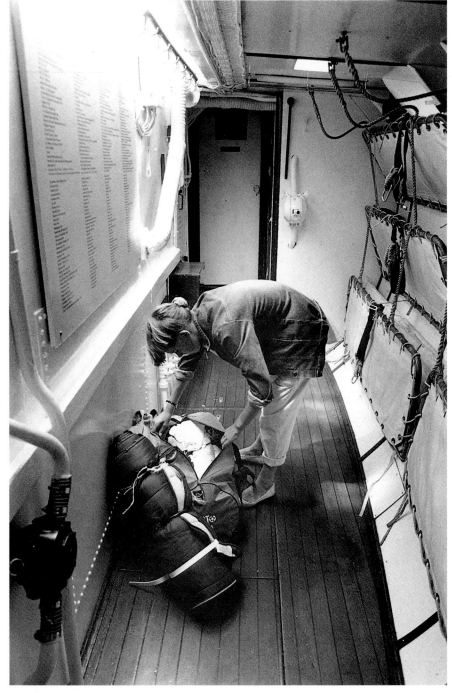

"Move only one hand or foot at a time so you keep three points of contact. Keep your hands on the verticals. Better not look down. Now reach up!" Encouraging advice from Lt. Cdr. Geoff Ulrich, captain of Royalist, *for a girl cadet laying aloft for the first time. Invariably the hardest bit is scrambling up and over the platform called the top, but the more "up and overs" you do, the easier it gets.*

Life on board a sailing ship is strange, quite hard, and certainly unlike anything ashore. First thing is to find your bunk and stow your gear. Young people come on board tense, awkward, and apprehensive, but in a few days the spirit among them will be so strong that they will feel they can put the ship on their shoulders and run with it.

"Will I really have to climb right up there?" A first-tripper aged thirteen casts an anxious glance aloft as he lines up on deck with his shipmates to hear the captain's welcome and briefing.

ABOVE: *Getting the feel of working aloft while the ship is still in smooth water, topmen lay out on the topsail yards for sail-furling drill under the eye of the sailing master and bos'n.*

BELOW: *"Don't cross your feet. Lean your tummy in and swing your feet back!" The whole purpose of going aloft is to do a job. Whatever they say about one hand for the ship and one for yourself, work aloft often* needs two hands. *Cadets learn how to find their balance on the footropes of the fore topsail yard.*

DAY TWO

ABOVE: "Messmen to the galley!" Every cadet takes a turn at helping the cook prepare the food, serving the officers at table, and washing dishes. In lively seas this can be harder than working on deck.

ABOVE: The real thing at last. Dipping into the waves, Royalist comes alive as she heads for the horizon. Cadets find their sea legs as they heave and haul. Wet ropes raise many a raw blister on soft hands.

RIGHT AND FAR RIGHT: The wind is strengthening, the jib is lowered. Now cadets in the deck-watch get an exciting roller coaster ride on the bowsprit. As they struggle to lash the sail down, green seas slosh through the safety netting.

DAY THREE

TOP LEFT: *The fundamental benefit of sail training is self-discovery. You find out how much you can do in rigorous conditions. The experience is difficult and testing. Not everybody enjoys it. But even if they hope never to do it again, few would miss it for the world. And nobody ever forgets it.*

ABOVE: *Seasickness is a miserable business but brings no dishonor. Even Lord Nelson suffered from seasickness, and look what happened to him! Nearly everybody suffers from it. What matters is how you cope with it. There are two stages. First you think you are going to die, then you hope you are.*

LEFT: *"That young man there! When I say pull, I want you to pull your heart out!" The rough edge of the sailing master's tongue is a fact of life. New hands have to take it in their stride, like spray in the face and cold water down the back of the neck.*

"Two, six, heave!" Putting their backs into it, cadets heave on a halyard. The traditional chant sung out to coordinate hauling on a rope is thought to have originated in Nelson's gun crews.

DAY FOUR

LEFT: *Sitting around the table in their quarters forward, cadets learn about the finer points of working ship and sail handling from the sailing master.*

BELOW: *Classes in seamanship continue while at sea. Every cadet works to improve his or her qualifications and can ultimately become a ship's watch leader.*

RIGHT: It's not long before hard pulling on wet ropes raises blisters and calluses. After a while, cadets forget the pain and proudly show off their "Cape Horn hands."

FAR RIGHT: Polishing, painting, scrubbing, cleaning, and polishing again. As always, sailors take pride in routine shipboard work. This kind of work was never so much fun at home!

BELOW: In training ships the world over, the scrubbing brush is the basic tool of seamanship, even more than the marline-spike. Decks are thoroughly scrubbed down at least once a day.

DAY FIVE

LEFT AND ABOVE: *A square-rigged sailing vessel in her hands, this young lass from Liverpool gets the hang of the wheel and keeps her eyes firmly fixed on the lubber's line in the compass.*

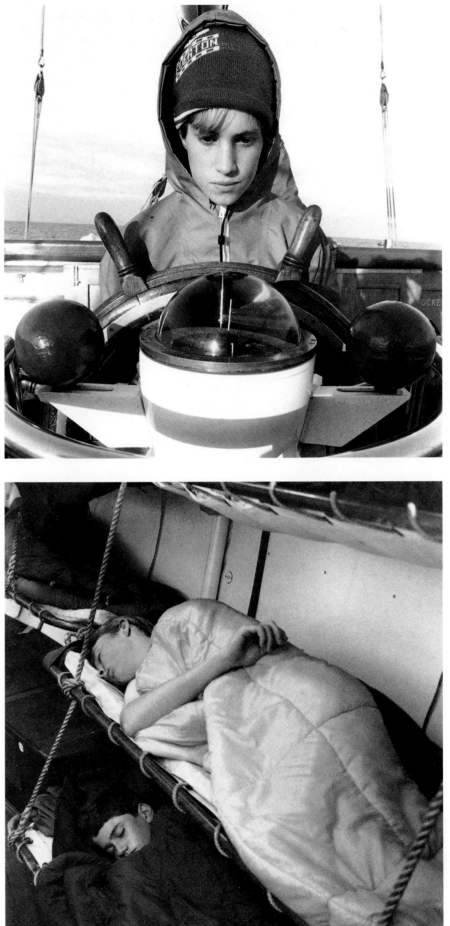

LEFT: *Waves smash over the deck, water sluices along the hull, footsteps stamp along the deck, ropes rattle, and sails thunder — but after five days of hard work and sea air the watch below is dead to the world.*

169

RIGHT: *"Steer two-one-zero degrees."*
"Two-one-zero degrees, aye aye, sir."
Under the eye of an officer, every cadet has
a spell on the wheel during watch on deck.

BELOW: *Seasick and exhausted but still on*
deck and ready to work when needed,
cadets find refuge wherever they can.

DAY SIX

LEFT: *Soon it seems you have never known any other life. The ship is your whole world. Everybody has been put through the wringer. Now they are emerging as hardy and useful sailors.*

BELOW: *Conquering fear, not giving up, doing your share of work and a bit more, living up to the demands of the ship — this is sail training.*

The smile at the end of the storm says
everything about sail training. It was a
hard trip. Nothing was easy and some of
it was a bit frightening. But it was an
experience nobody will ever forget and
most will sign up again.

TALL SHIPS RACES

A TALL SHIPS Race typically covers about six hundred sea miles and lasts up to six days, though transatlantic legs are much longer. A support vessel such as a naval frigate accompanies the fleet and makes radio contact with every vessel at least once daily for safety checks.

At the end of a race every vessel's elapsed time is adjusted with a rating, or handicap, called a time correction factor. The rating is a formula carefully calculated (and kept secret to avoid loopholes being exploited) to give all vessels an equal chance of winning, whatever their size, rig, and crew. The biggest and most powerful ship may be first to cross the finishing line, but the race actually will be won by the vessel putting on the best performance in relation to its size.

With such a disparity of vessels in the competition — large and small, fast and slow, new and old — the fleet becomes very spread out. Every race has a time limit to ensure the tail-enders do not miss the festivities and intership visits in port. Those still at sea when the race ends are not disqualified. For a group of youngsters slaving to drive some heavy old vessel, it would be unnecessarily hard luck to be eliminated just because they had run out of time. Instead, their positions are recorded and speeds up to that moment are calculated. Then all are compared to find the winner. It sometimes happens that a vessel which has not actually crossed the finishing line is declared the winner, an occurrence that reveals something of the spirit of sportsmanship in Tall Ships Races.

The "family" — the world total of sail-training vessels — is thought to number about six hundred. Of these, 381 bear the letters TS on their sails, signifying that they are associated with the Sail Training Association. For racing, they are grouped in three main classes:

CLASS A   All square-riggers, including the big and eye-catching ships, barques, barquentines, brigs, and brigantines, are Class A vessels. They total 34 vessels and fly the flags of 22 countries. Nearly all are owned or sponsored by governments. They carry large complements and sail to train naval, merchant marine, fishery, or coast guard cadets in basic seamanship. Classes continue at sea, even during races.

In some races, square-riggers of less than 120 feet in overall length are classed as Class A, Division II.

CLASS B   Class B comprises schooners and other fore-and-aft rigged vessels longer than 100 feet but smaller than 160 feet on the waterline. These vessels carry small crews on short voyages, and emphasize participation, team spirit, and adventure rather than training for a career at sea.

CLASS C   Yachts and others vessels less than 100 feet overall are considered Class C craft. In most races these are further separated into two or three divisions. Any vessel longer than 30 feet on the waterline may participate in Tall Ships Races run by the STA as long as more than half its complement is aged between sixteen and twenty-five and is on board for the purpose of sail training.

The large Class C fleet includes vessels run by clubs, societies, schools, military organizations, and individuals. About half are vessels of the traditional type while the remainder are yachts less than ten years old.

TALL SHIPS IN COMMISSION

LENGTH MEASUREMENTS refer to the maximum length of a ship's hull (bowsprit not included). Unless stated otherwise, ship-rigged vessels and barques have three masts and schooners have two.

CLASS A (All square-rigged vessels longer than 120 ft. and all other vessels longer than 160 ft.)

Danmark, ship rig, 253 ft., built 1933 for training Danish Merchant Marine, complement 92.

Georg Stage, ship rig, 151 ft., built 1935 to train merchant navy cadets of Denmark, complement 71.

Amerigo Vespucci, ship rig, 266 ft., built 1931 for Italian Navy, complement about 400.

Statsraad Lehmkuhl, barque, 276 ft., built 1914, now school ship of Bergen, Norway, now being restored; complement about 100.

Christian Radich, ship rig, 205 ft., built 1937 as school ship for Oslo and eastern Norway, complement 94.

Sorlandet, ship rig, 185 ft., built 1927, now school ship of Kristiansand, Norway, complement about 100.

Gorch Fock II, barque, 285 ft., built 1958 for German Navy, complement about 190.

Eagle, barque, 265 ft., built 1936, now serving United States Coast Guard, complement about 190.

Sagres II, barque, 267 ft., built 1937, now Portuguese Navy, complement about 190.

Tovarisch, barque, 263 ft., built 1933, now Navy of USSR, complement about 220.

Lord Nelson, barque, 141 ft., built 1986 in Great Britain and specially fitted so half her 40 crew may have physical disabilities; even the bowsprit is accessible by wheelchair; berths are available for people of all ages and nationalities.

Belem, barque, 200 ft., built 1886, as a cocoa-bean carrier, later used to train orphans as seamen in Venice, restored in France 1985, complement about 70.

Kruzenshtern, 4-mast barque, 342 ft., now Fisheries Board of USSR, 80 crew and 161 cadets.

Sedov, 4-mast barque, 385 ft., now Fisheries Board of USSR, 70 crew and 140 cadets.

Mircea, barque, 239 ft., built 1939, now merchant marine of Romania, complement about 200.

Dar Mlodziezy, ship rig, 298 ft., built 1980 for Polish Merchant Marine Academy, complement about 250.

Juan Sebastian de Elcano, 4-mast topsail schooner, 304 ft., built 1927 for Navy of Spain, complement 330.

Libertad, ship rig, 298 ft., built 1956 for Navy of Argentina, complement 390.

Esmeralda, 4-mast barquentine, 309 ft., built 1952 for Navy of Chile, complement 300.

Gloria, barque, 249 ft., built 1968 for Navy of Colombia, complement about 150.

Guayas, barque, 257 ft., built 1976 for Navy of Ecuador, complement about 150.

Simon Bolivar, barque, 270 ft., built 1980 for Navy of Venezuela, complement about 170.

Cuauhtemoc, barque, 297 ft., built 1982 for Navy of Mexico, complement 175.

Capitan Miranda, three-masted staysail schooner, 205 ft., built 1930 for cargo, remodeled 1977 for Navy of Uruguay, complement 85.

Nippon Maru, 4-mast barque, 282 ft., built 1984 for Merchant Marine of Japan, complement about 200.

Kaiwo Maru, 4-mast barque, 307 ft., built 1930 for Merchant Marine of Japan, complement about 200.

Grossherzogin Elisabeth, 3-mast schooner, 167 ft., built 1909, now training cadets for merchant navy of West Germany, complement about 60.

Dewarutji, barquentine, 191 ft., built 1953 for navy of Indonesia, complement 102.

Elissa, barque, 160 ft., built 1877, a working vessel until 1975 when bought as a sailing museum ship for Galveston, Texas.

Gazela of Philadelphia, barquentine, 186 ft., built 1883, last survivor of the Portuguese square-rigged fishing fleet, now used in sail training from Philadelphia, complement 55.

CLASS A, DIVISION II   (Square-rigged vessels less than 120 ft. overall hull length)

Royalist, brig, 76 ft., built 1971 for the Sea Cadet Corps of Great Britain, complement 40.

Varuna, brig, twin of *Royalist*, trains young people in India, complement about 40.

Asgard II, brigantine, 87 ft., built 1979 for the Sail Training Association of Ireland, complement 25.

CLASS B   (Fore-and-aft rigged vessels between 100 ft. and 160 ft. length overall.)

Bluenose II, 143 ft., schooner, replica of Grand Banks fishing schooner, built 1963 for Province of Nova Scotia, Canada, complement 17.

Falken, Gladan, schooners, 112 ft., built 1946 and 1947 for Swedish Navy, complement 42.

Sir Winston Churchill, Malcolm Miller, 3-mast topsail schooners, 134 ft., built 1966 ·and 1968 for Sail Training Association of Great Britain, complement 40.

L'Etoile, La Belle Poule, topsail schooners, 99 ft., built 1932 for French Navy, complement 50.

Eendracht, schooner, 107 ft., built 1974 for Sail Training Association of the Netherlands, complement 37.

Fulton, 3-mast topsail schooner, 92 ft., former coaster now sailing for National Museum of Denmark, complement about 40.

Pogoria, barquentine, 134 ft., built 1980 for Iron Shackle Fraternity of Poland, complement about 55.

Kaliakra, barquentine, 134 ft., sister ship of *Pogoria*, built 1986 to train cadets for merchant marine of Bulgaria, complement about 55.

Zawisza Czarny, 3-mast staysail schooner, 120 ft., built 1952, now sailed by Polish Pathfinders Union, complement 56.

Elinor, barquentine, 118 ft., built 1906, owned in Denmark, complement about 18.

Shabab Oman, 3-mast topsail schooner, 144 ft., built 1971, now sailed by youth of Oman, complement 48.

Spirit of Adventure, topsail schooner, 84 ft., built 1973 for sail training in New Zealand, complement 34

Spirit of New Zealand, barquentine, 125 ft., built 1986 for sail training in New Zealand, complement 51.

Ji Fung, brigantine, 130 ft., sailed by Outward Bound in Hong Kong, complement 50.

ACKNOWLEDGMENTS

This book would not have been possible without the friendly and hospitable assistance of the captains, officers, crews, and all our shipmates during the ocean passages we made in the vessels now sailing the pages of this book. It was a challenge for us to do justice to the high standards of leadership and seamanship with which today's sail-training vessels are operated. Above all, it has been a privilege to share something of that unique bond that grows between shipmates: the spirit of sail.

In particular, we would like to express our gratitude to the governments of Argentina, Federal Republic of Germany, Poland, Portugal, and the United States of America for allowing one or both of us to sail in their training ships; also to the Sea Cadet Corps of Great Britain and the Sail Training Association of the Netherlands.

We owe a special debt to John Hamilton and officers of the Sail Training Association in Great Britain, Captain George Crowninshield of the American Sail Training Association, and Oliver Pemberton of Cutty Sark. For helpful technical advice we thank Captain Ernst Cummings and Lieutenant Edwin Daniels of the USCG barque *Eagle*, and Richard Birchall of Toronto Brigantine, besides the many sailors whose friendly conversations during lonely sea-watches gave us an insight into the realities of the most romantic of vessels—the Tall Ship.

A great number of books were consulted in the process of background research for the text. In particular, John Dyson acknowledges his debt to the following: Frank T. Bullen, *The Cruise of the Cachalot* (New York 1928). George Campbell, *China Tea Clippers* (London 1974). Joseph Conrad, *Mirror of the Sea* (London 1923). Francis Chichester, *Along the Clipper Way* (London 1966). Arthur H. Clark, *The Clipper Ship Era* (New York 1910). Neale Haley, *The Schooner Era* (New York 1972). Holly Hollins, *The Tall Ships Are Sailing* (London 1982). Henry Hughes, *Immortal Sails* (Prescot 1977). A.A. Hurst, *The Call of High Canvas* (London 1958). William H.S. Jones, *The Cape Horn Breed* (London 1956). Basil Lubbock, *Round the Horn before the Mast* (London 1902); *The China Clippers* (Glasgow 1925); *The Last of the Windjammers* (Glasgow 1927). David R. McGregor, *The Tea Clippers* (London 1972); *Clipper Ships* (London 1979); *Schooners in Four Centuries* (London 1982); *Merchant Sailing Ships 1850–1875* (London 1984). George Putz, *Eagle, America's Sailing Square Rigger* (Chester, Conn., 1986). Frank H. Shaw, *White Sails and Spindrift* (London 1946). Alan Villiers, *The Way of a Ship* (London 1952); *By Way of Cape Horn* (London 1952); *Of Ships and Men* (London 1962).

Peter Christopher
John Dyson
1987